AF476962

JEN RAY

AIN'T WE GOT FUN

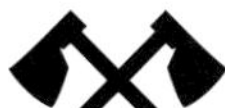

gestalten

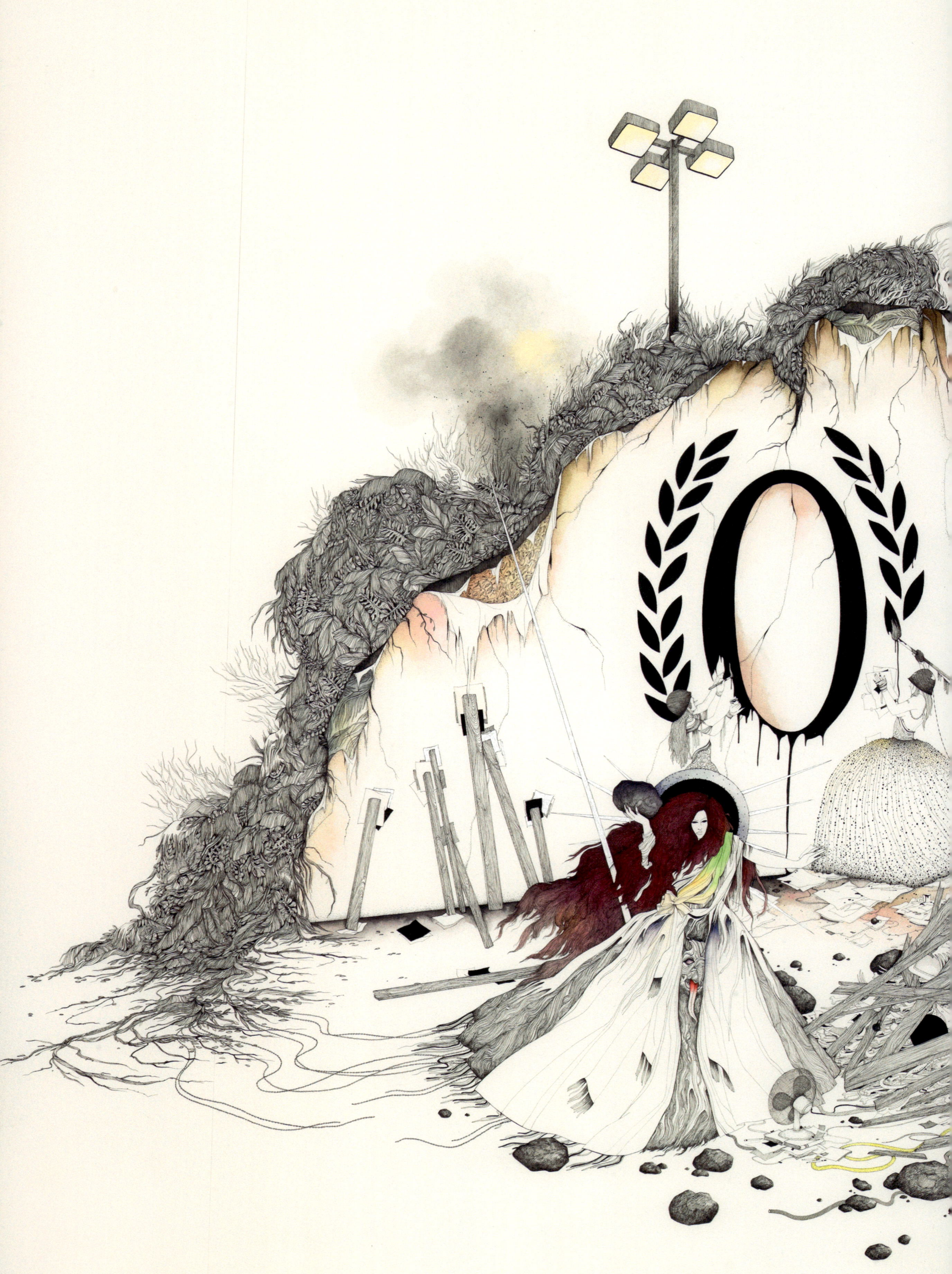

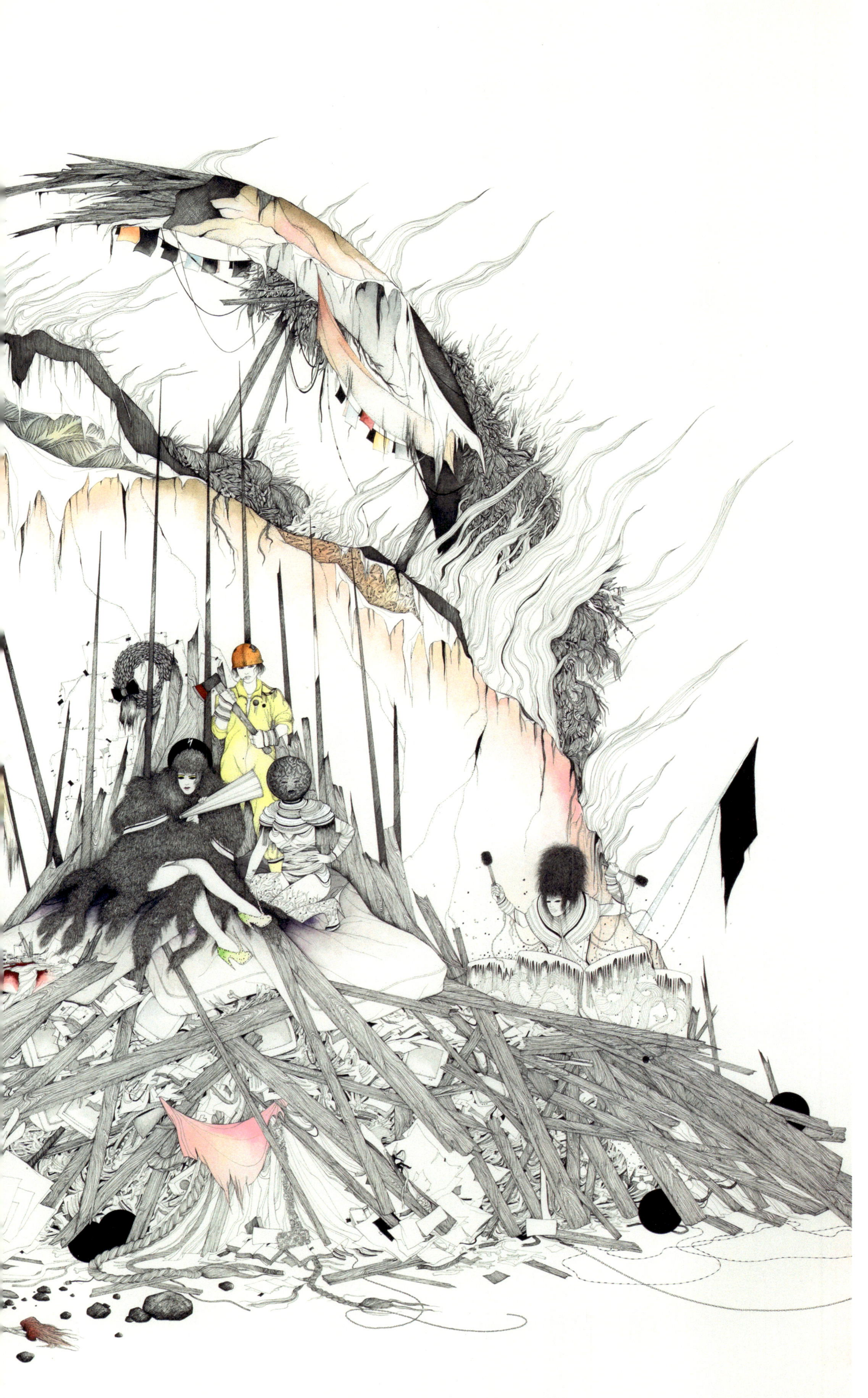

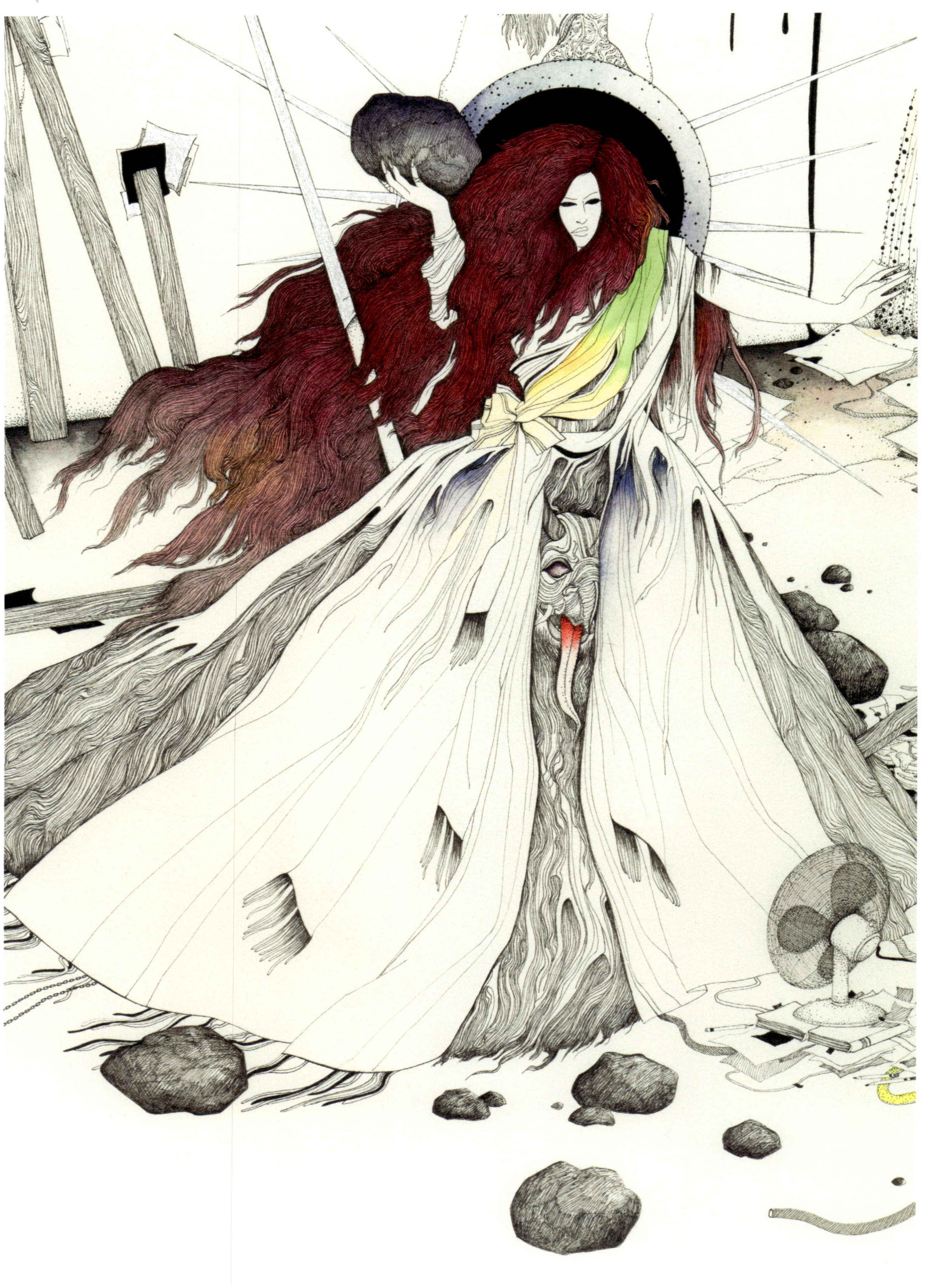

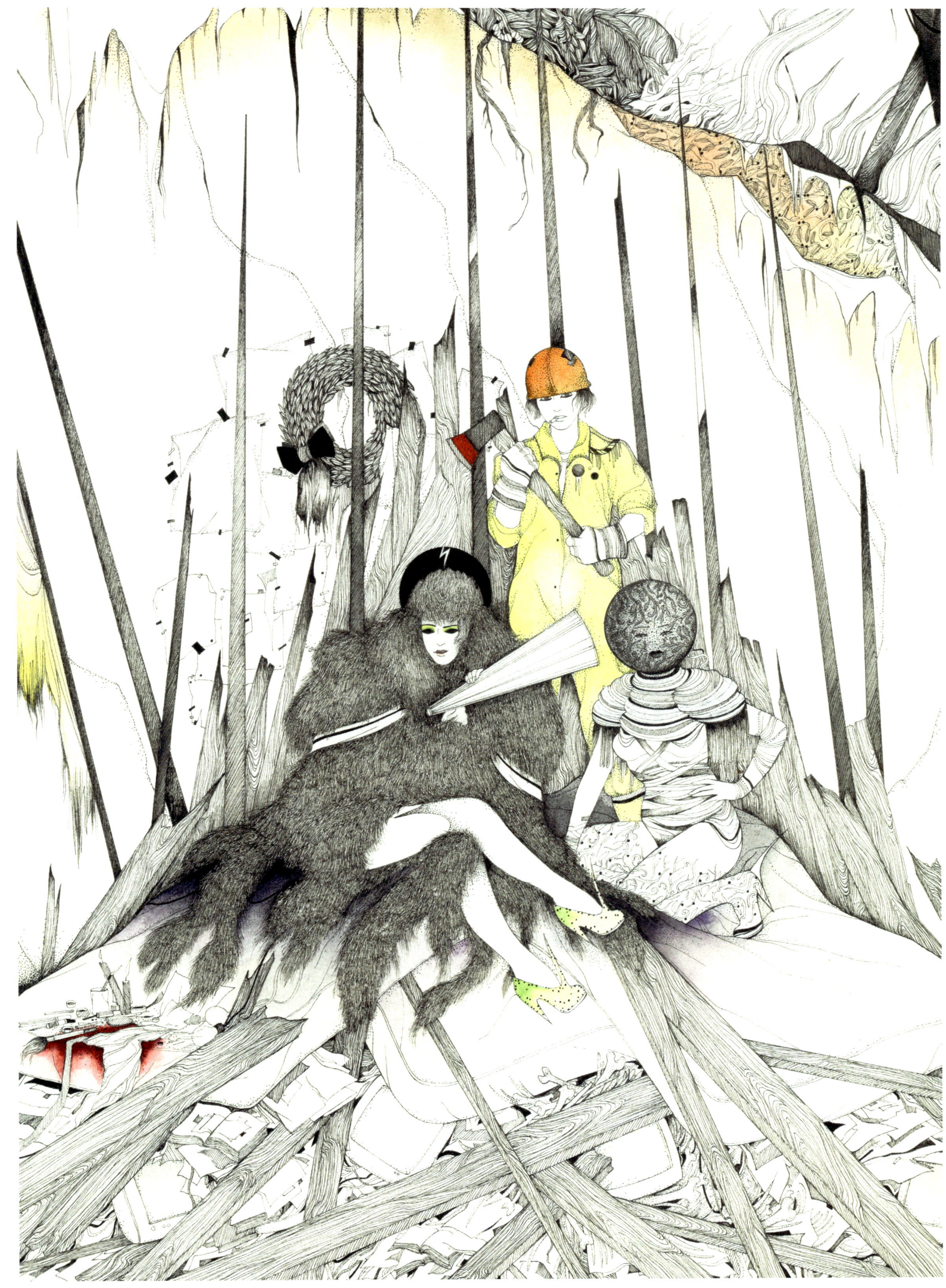

GOD~DESSES ON THE RAM~PAGE

ESSAY BY ROBBERT ROOS

In our postmodern times, eclecticism is the norm. Artists appropriate, collage, assemble, sample, quote, and mix freely. But it is not only art history in which artists shop. If anything, the scope for artistic inspiration has widened immensely, ever since the sixties, when "low culture" became fashionable. Of course there have been more eclectic periods in art history – most notably the neo-movements – but they themselves more or less developed into a proper identifiable "style." Not so in contemporary art. The phrase "anything goes" that was popularized in the eighties, still applies, but contrary to the belief that "anything goes" (or better "I have complete freedom") reflects an emptiness or a lack of conceptual thinking; the free quotation from multi-layered sources is a valid position to evaluate the immense archive of images and information compiled in our mass media world. To the encyclopedia of art history, one can add the whole thesaurus of visual culture as it developed in the 20th century, including the more "popular" disciplines like design, fashion, comics, movies, and advertisement.

It is in this framework that Jen Ray finds her place. In her drawings, classic mythology meets Star Wars meets seventies glamrock meets art deco fashion design meets critical feminist thinking meets the burlesque of the thirties meets comic strips.

Forget Anakin. Forget Luke Skywalker. Enter Princess Leia Organa as the superhero-protagonist of an epic battle. With Jen Ray at the helm of a fantasy ride – and not George Lucas – this change from supporting role to center stage for a female warrior is more than just an illusion. In Ray's world, women rule the battlefield. Immediately the mind goes back to the legendary Amazons, the army of Penthesilea cum suis, who roamed around in the mythical world.

According to some historians the myth of the Amazons was an invention of the patriarchal Greeks to create a nightmarish parable in which they could warn against women who would become too strong. A tale of war – the comfortable habitat of "real men" – was the ultimate podium to teach a moral lesson. By taming and killing the "barbaric" women – Hercules would do this by ultimately defeating the Amazons to steal the golden girdle of Hippolyte – the Greeks sent the message that natural order will always be restored. This makes the Amazon tale an early example of gender profiling. In the 19th century this take on the story was further enhanced by the German playwright Heinrich von Kleist. He wrote a tragedy involving Penthesilea and Achilles, which ends up as a brutal ritual dance full of lust, sex, and violence. Von Kleist's interpretation is a violent tale bordering on sado-masochism.

The complexity of the various layers within the story of the Amazons provides an ideal playground for Jen Ray's artistic explorations. Her work deals with femininity in a proud, almost matter-of-fact way. Her elaborate landscapes are only inhabited by women. That is, if we look at the human figures. There are males in the scenery, but they are always disguised as animals. Ray understands that contrasting the female energy with a "male force" strengthens the equilibrium of the total picture.

As any female artist dealing with gender issues, Jen Ray cannot escape the work of the feminist artists of the seventies. Artists like Hannah Wilke and Carolee Schneemann were not afraid to use their own body as a means of expression. Porn was re-contextualized by women as a power to express their own pleasure. The writer Valerie Solanas came up with the SCUM Manifesto: a radical way to have the whole gender issue solved by promoting a completely matriarchal society. She writes: "SCUM – dominant, secure, self-confident, nasty, violent, selfish, independent, proud, thrill-seeking, free-wheeling, arrogant females, who consider themselves fit to rule the universe, who have free-wheeled to the limits of this "society" and are ready to wheel on to something far beyond what it has to offer." It could be a description of the women in Jen Ray's drawings, were it not for the slightly derailed destructive nature that lay behind Solanas's writing. In 1968 Solanas gained notoriety with her attack on Andy Warhol.

Stylistically, Jen Ray can also be linked to another artist from that time: Dorothy Iannone. In recent years Iannone has come to the forefront again, with a rediscovery of her work. It centers around a message of love, sex, spirituality, body, and soul. The idiom of Iannone is based on a self-taught drawing technique that favors a strong line in a more or less "descriptive," almost cartoon-like style. Elegant, proud women show off their sexuality as goddesses in paintings decorated like an Egyptian tomb with signs of lust and love.

Jen Ray mixes Solanas and Iannone in a vocabulary completely of her own. What catches the eye first is the endlessly refined detailing in the large-scale, panoramic scenes. The boldness of the grand compositions is breathtaking, because it is done with such meticulous precision. The complexity of the total scene entertains at first sight. The power of the detail engages a second, third, even fourth look.

In a typical drawing – "Untitled (Second Double)" (p.44) – we see a battlefield. Two ship-like elevated platforms are at the center of the scene, both inhabited by women wearing helmets, waving battle flags with a variety of signs. Some women wear heavily decorated masks, mimicking great Indian chiefs. The structures tower over pointed rocks, a large heap – the size of a mountain – containing wreaths, books, pamphlets, bones, even chairs, tires and uniforms. In the middle of the heap a woman – with a soul-like hairdo straight from the seventies – poses like a sexy free spirit on a chair. On the pointed rocks a female warrior raises a red pointed sword. Victory! A Roman wreath on a spear standing in the heap of bones is a remnant of the battle that was won. The whole scene has at first an archaic character. Until you see a Howitzer cannon on the left, and a car being toppled over by a group of females on the right. And not to forget three women in the right side of the picture skyrocketing through the air like science fiction warriors. One of the females is sitting guard by some rubble that includes destroyed computers. And on and on it goes. The more you look, the more details pop up. When you think you have the scene sorted out, something new catches your eyes to unsettle your reading of it.

This is where the eclecticism kicks in. We go from Roman battlefields to destructive street scenes befitting a ghetto to the fictitious battlegrounds of science fiction. The distinctive personal drawing style is a mix of elegant art deco lines (and matching use of expressive watercolors), comic strip imagery, classic pen drawing techniques, and the clear-cut atmosphere of Japanese Ukiyo-e woodcuts, adorned with a touch of seventies hallucination. Despite the critical undercurrents in the scenes, they are light footed as well. Ray mixes mythology with social criticism with postmodern irony with hedonistic popular culture.

The list of references that you can distill from the pictures is nearly endless. Ray's Amazons could be personages from burlesque cabaret revues in the Weimar Republic, actresses from big show ballets in Hollywood films of the thirties (remember the grand choreographies of Busby Berkeley), or dancers in the erotic shows of the Crazy Horse nightclub in Paris. The scenes radiate decadence, but also neutral rationalism. There is the pumped up neo-Gothic imagery or the almost mathematical repetitive composition scheme of a painter like Paolo Uccello. And there are all the references to military iconography: the parades, the uniforms, the flags,

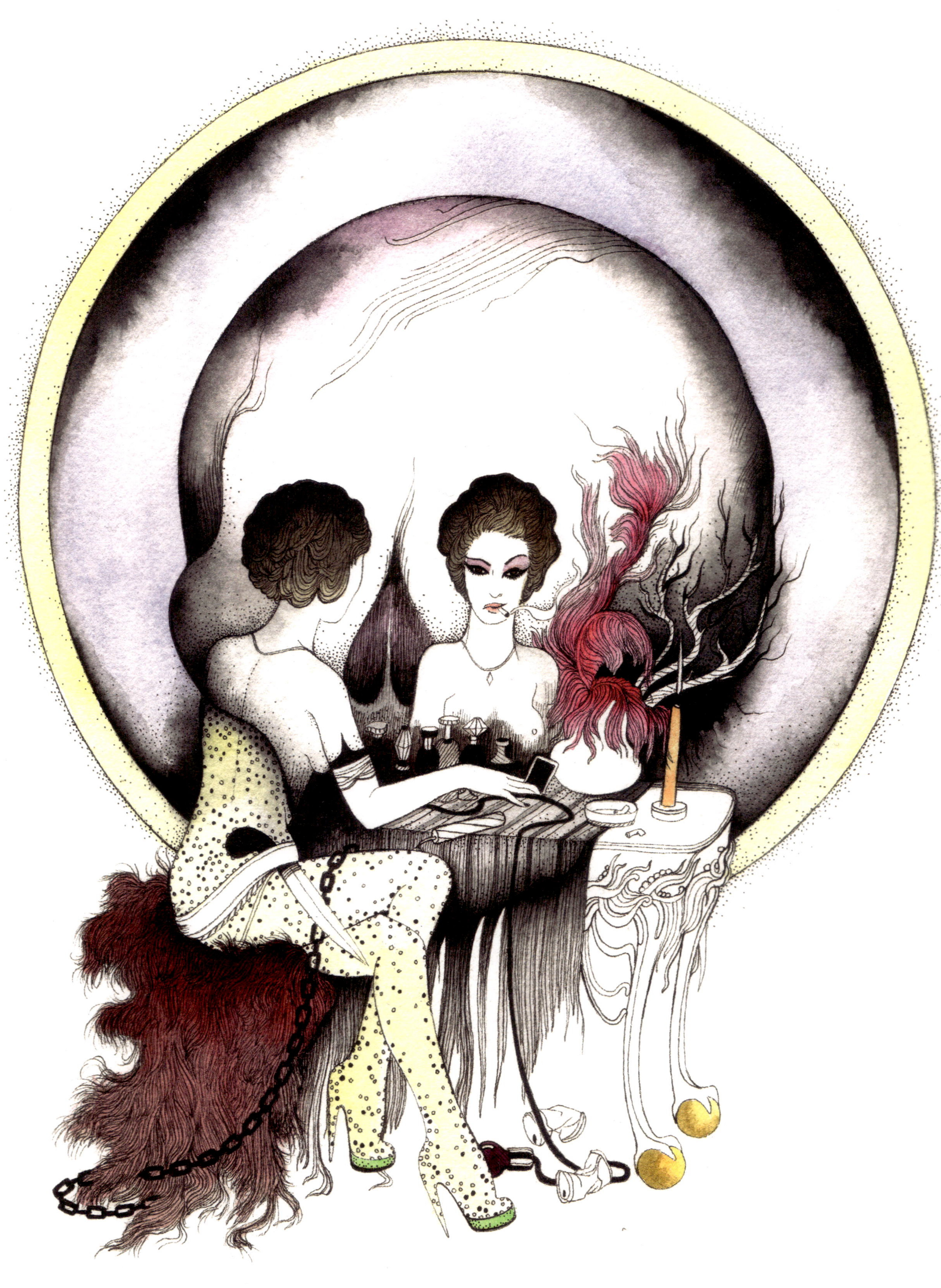

the weaponry, the formations, the idea of battle itself. But also these aspects are juxtaposed with everyday, popular themes like carnival, homecoming parades, gay pride extravaganza, and floats.

The drawings of Jen Ray are the epitome of a tableau vivant. The idea of the tableau vivant mixes the theatrics of stage theater with the narrative qualities of a historical scene. "Dressing up" and role-playing are a strong part of the pictorial style. Especially in the 19th century – the Victorian era in England – this form of art was very popular, but also in the earlier 20th century there are great examples. Photographers were very much drawn to the concept.

The idea of the tableau vivant was a perfect cover to enact erotic scenes in the dark moral age of Queen Victoria. Look at the elaborate nude scenes in the works of the pre-Raphaelites, who based themselves on the romantic stories of great poets and writers. In France the tableau vivant can be recognized in the big heroic battle scenes that where depicted by 18th and 19th century French artists as Poussin, Gericault, and David, mimicking the classic battlefields. In the early 20th century, the dress up aspect of the tableau vivant – or role playing – was taken full advantage of by the surrealist artists. Up to cross dressing and playing with gender issues.

Dressing up and the theatrics of a grand epic story are two components Jen Ray clearly enjoys. In one of her most recent drawings she steps up the level of detail and complexity by deconstructing the stages of action over seven different platforms floating in the air like spaceships. In the middle is a hellish fire, rising up from raised spears held by unseen warriors beneath the picture frame. In the middle of the fire is a red skull adorned with wreath-like leaves, encapsulated in a blue sphere. Next to it is a platform with a half raised phallus-like obelisk, a potent erotic reference to manhood (albeit derelict). On a platform close-by, an astronaut inspects an oil barrel with pink smoke coming out of it. Two half dressed female warriors accompany her. One of two other platforms, a little further to the right, is engulfed in flames. A group of women stand guard in the middle with a banner behind them. A giant megaphone points towards the middle of the drawing. A lantern pole towers above the platform and lights it. On the second, smaller platform sits a shell-like cabin that echoes a strange, Jeroen Bosch-shaped creature. A warrior climbs from it with a rope.

As if all these elements weren't puzzling enough, the eyes drift to the left side of the picture, where a gigantic airship floats. A kind of rock singer seems to be at the helm. It is facing towards a platform at the left side of the fire. On this stage is a queen-like figure, dressed in an enormous cape (a reference to Freddie Mercury?) and next to her a huge portrait covered with an African mask, flanked by two green-clad ladies. The floor of the platform is covered with a tunic, candles, plates, forks, and bones. Someone had a great meal there.

The whole scene is a riddle. But logic isn't per se important. The drawings of Jen Ray are a perfect vehicle to make up your own stories. With of course the components of women heroes, gender issues, and a ritual dance between the chaos of destruction and decay and the power of victory as a promise of rebuilding. One detail in the above described drawing is only noticed by people who really look closely. Right at the bottom of the inferno is a small sign on a chain closing off the mouth of the fire that reads: piss off. As if Ray wants to say: hey, I warned you, enter this drawing at your own risk.

Out of a range of artists that you could pinpoint as references for the work of Jen Ray a couple stand out. The first is Henry Darger. He was a self-taught artist (1892-1973) living in Chicago, who worked in total anonymity for decades, producing panoramic drawings featuring hybrid girls-with-penises in grand battlefield scenes. Dargers intricate compositions – produced by copying source material in various sizes – have been an inspiration for many artists. The complexity and sometimes ambiguity of the scenes – with fairy tale elements – are an interesting match with Jen Ray's drawings.

Another artist that is in Jen Ray's realm is Marcel Dzama. In his drawings you see uniformed people in theatrical settings, with an undercurrent of violence, eroticism, and subtle irony. These are the same ingredients that Jen Ray plays with, even though the drawing styles are distinctly different.

To get closer to the drawing style of Ray we should look at Erté, an important reference. Erté was the chief fashion illustrator for the magazine *Harper's Bazaar* in the twenties and thirties. He also designed costumes and stages for the Paris nightclub Folies Bergère. He almost singlehandedly created the archetypical image of the modern, glamorous women of his time. They are slender, sharply lined, almost androgynous, but still distinctly female, elegant, and slightly mysterious (or diva-like). They wear colorful, lyrical clothes (bordering on extravagance), which makes them look exotic and romantic. Just like Jen Ray's women, Erté's are worldly and feminine, sexy and strong, elegant and exotic, everything at the same time. Multiple layers, multiple interpretations.

Jen Ray takes the tableau vivant as a pictorial style one step further by actually "staging" her drawings in large scale performances. For one, "Double Action", she teamed up with the Dutch artist Mathilde ter Heijne. With her performances Ray translates her fantasy world into a much sharper realism. Again the thirties come to mind, the interbellum period that saw the birth of two distinctive artistic movements: Dada/surrealism and the Berlin-based Neue Sachlichkeit. Both movements are reflected in Jen Ray's work: the absurdist, rather disruptive look at society with strong sexual undercurrents of the surrealists and the more politically motivated mocking of social archetypes in the work of Berliners like Georg Grosz, Otto Dix, and Hannah Höch. Several styles and cultural movements intermix in the entrancing drawings and performances of Jen Ray. Eclectic. In the best, multilayered sense of the word.

Robbert Roos
Chief Curator Kunsthal KAdE at Amersfoort, The Netherlands

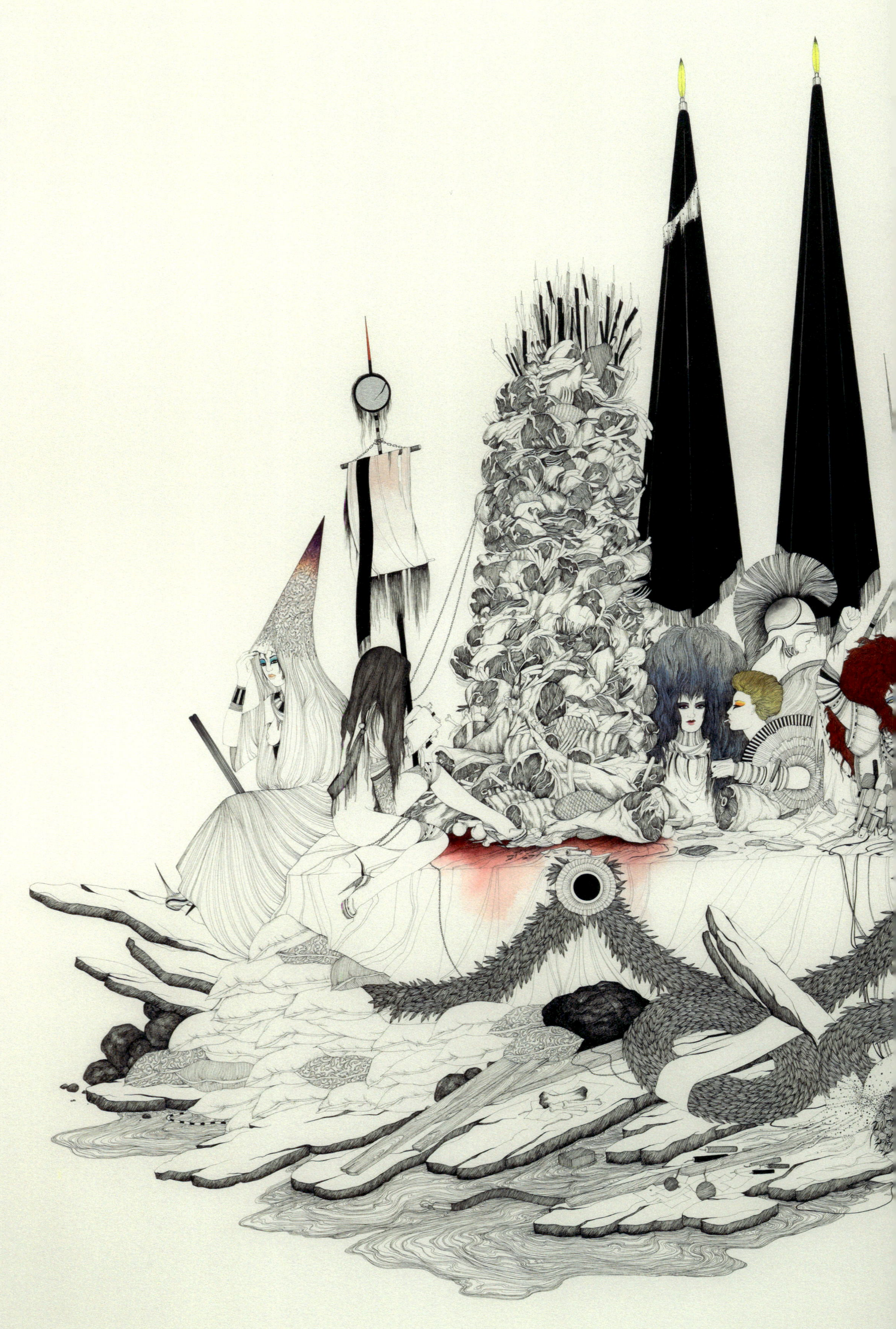

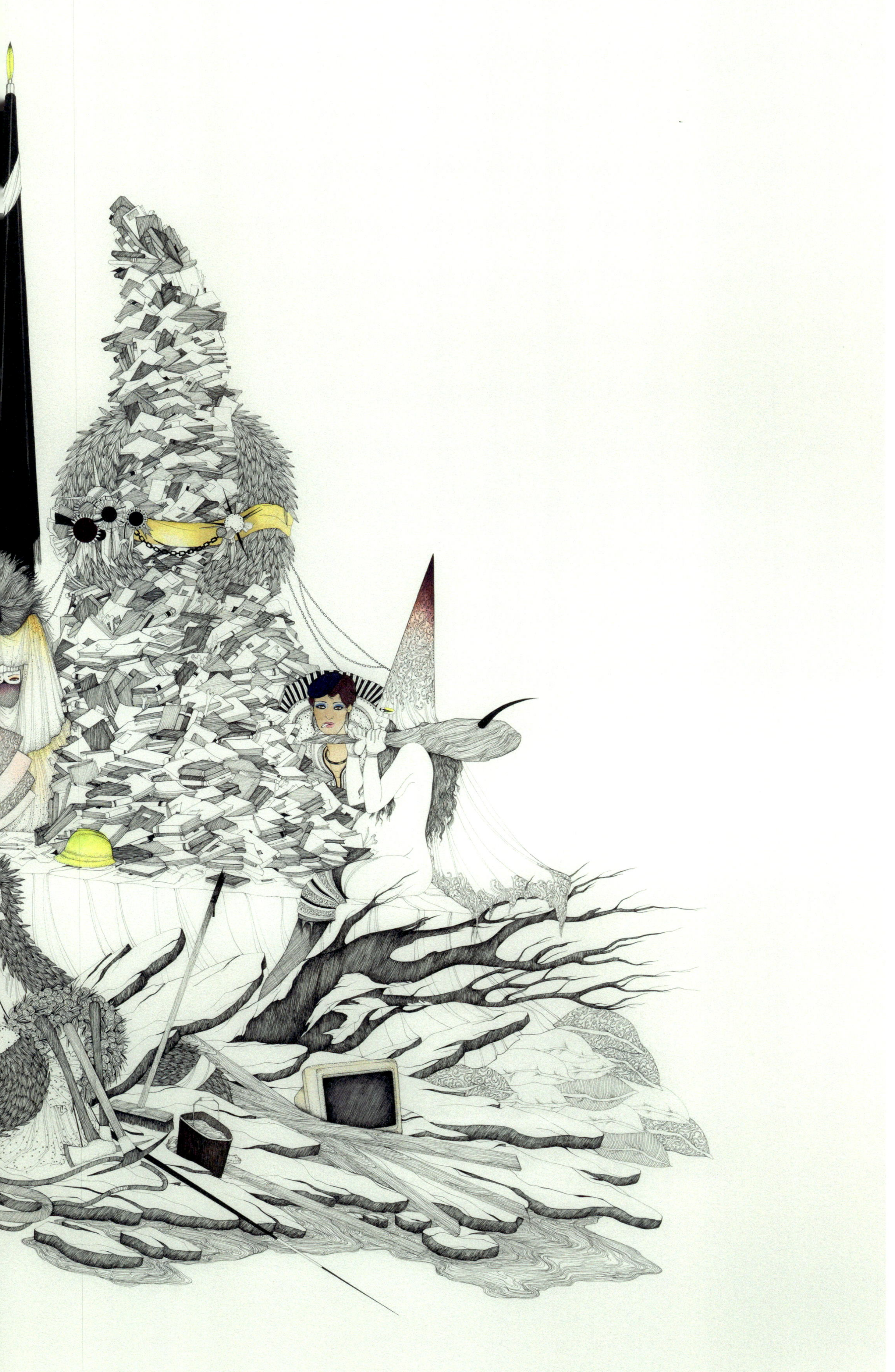

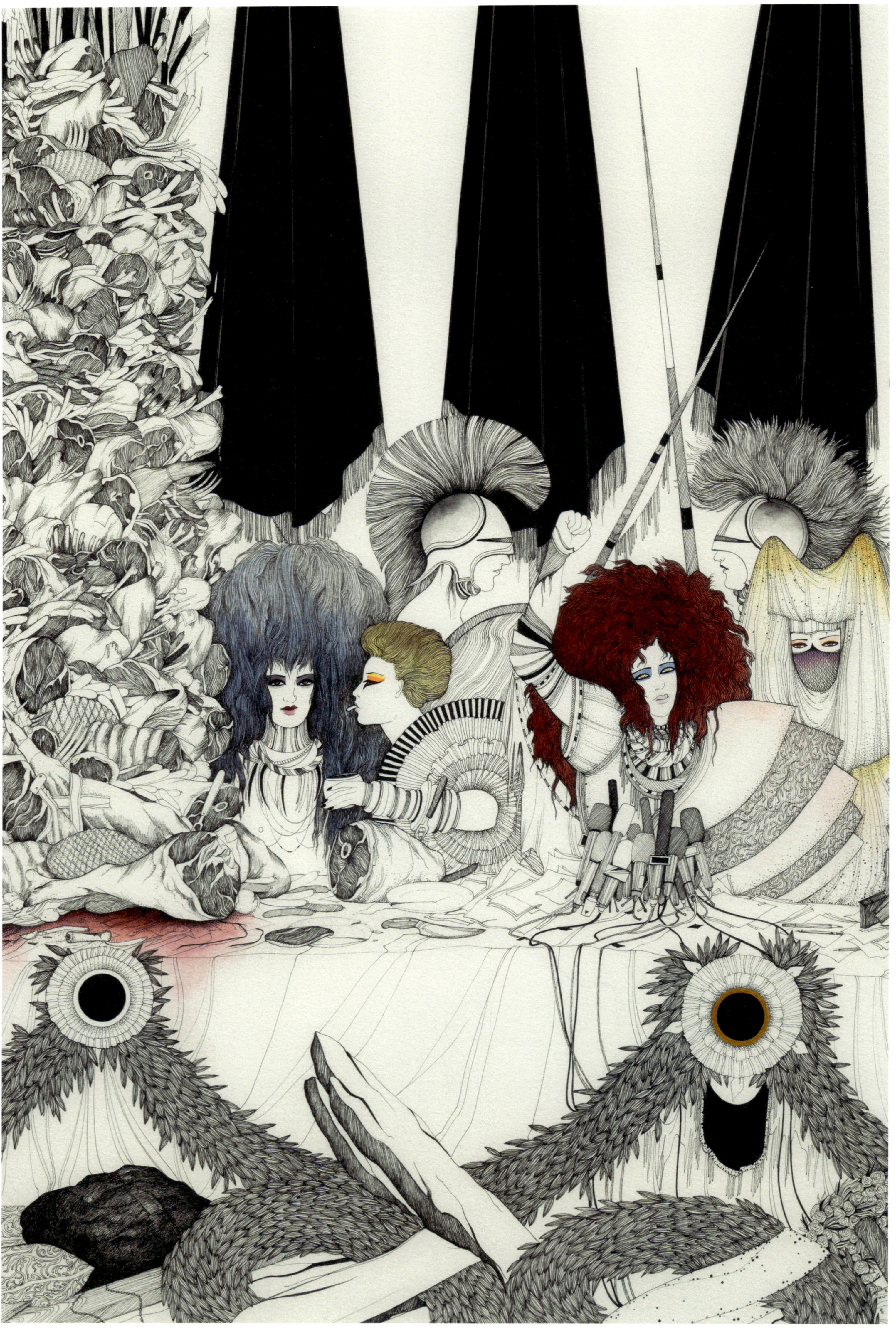

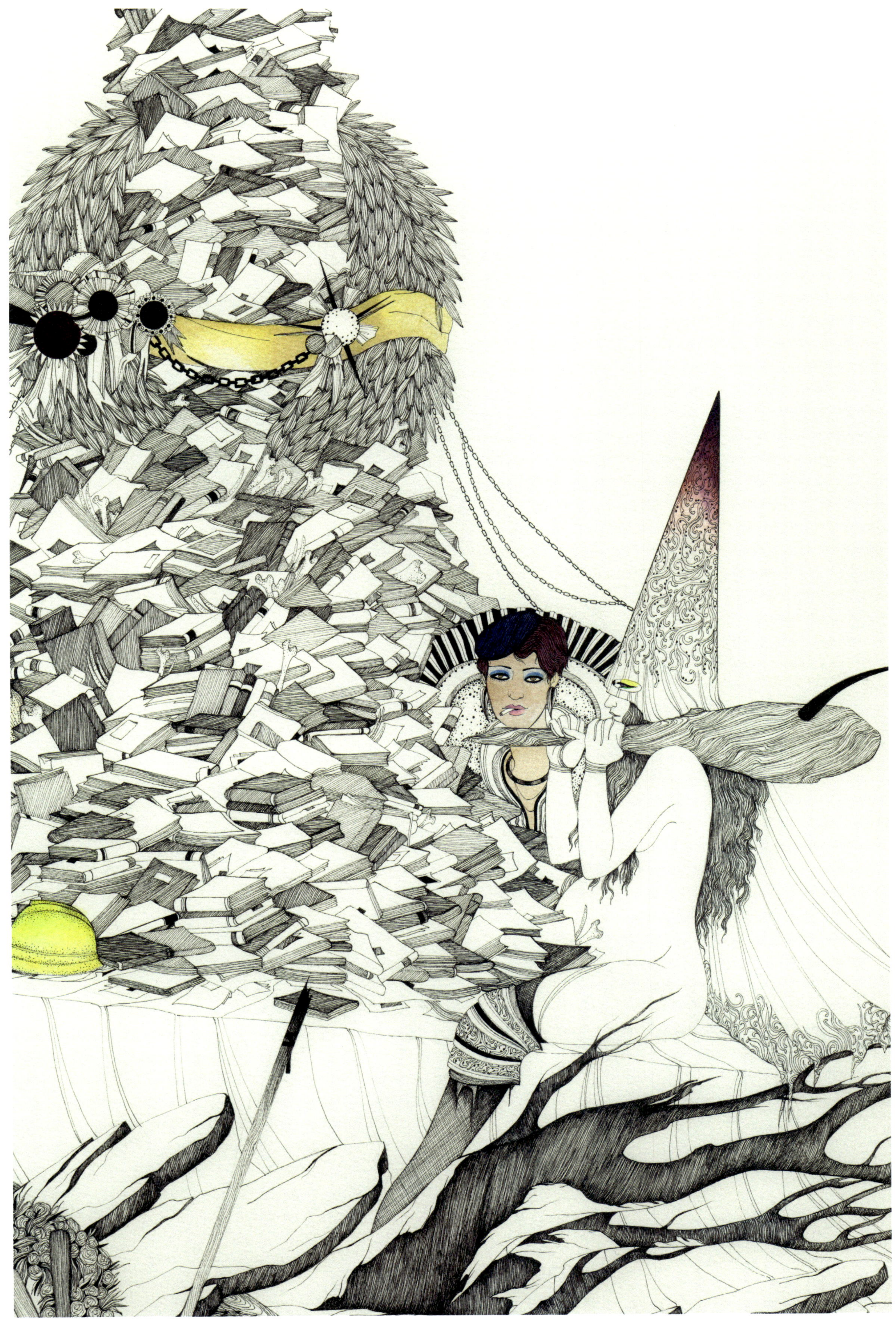

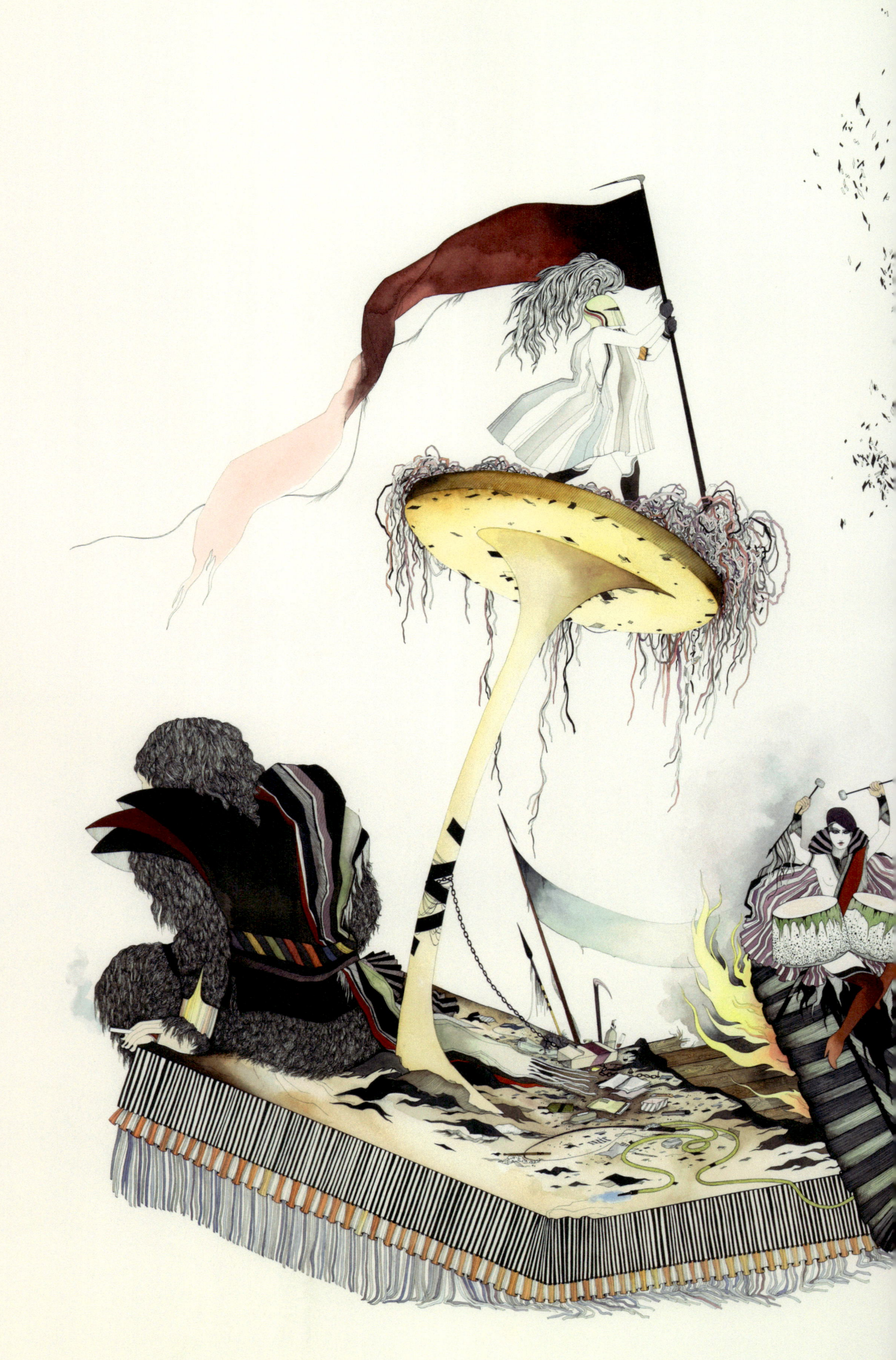

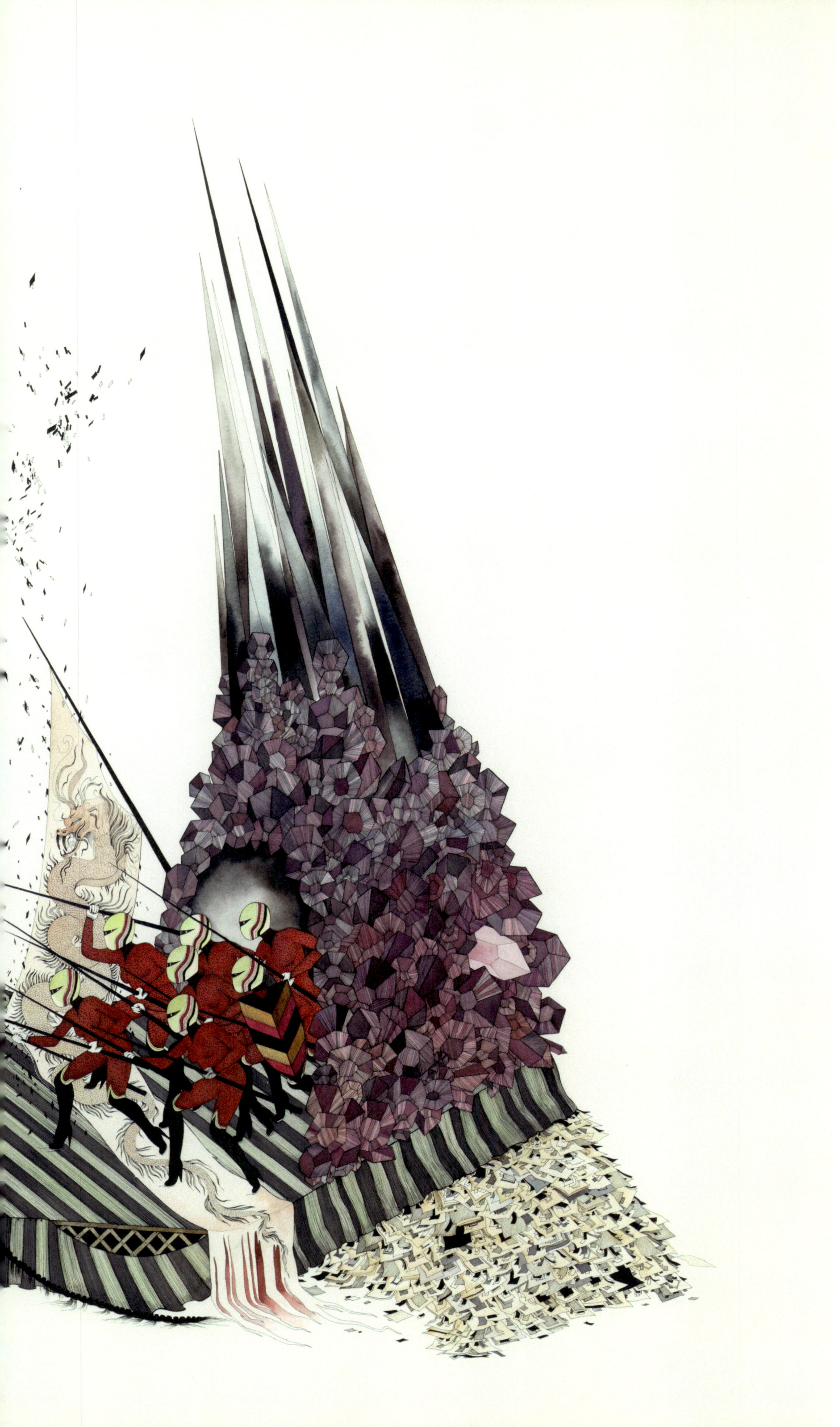

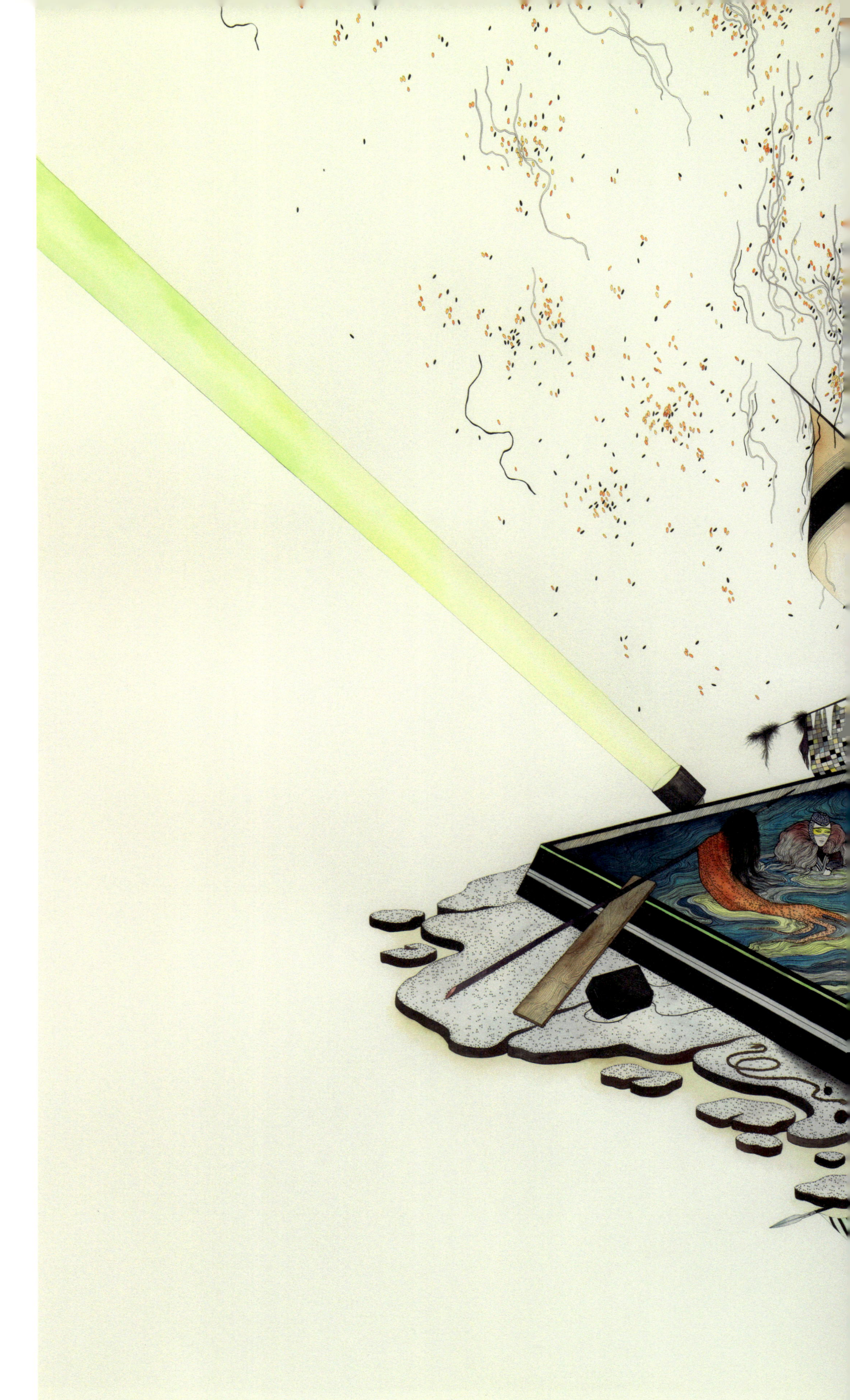

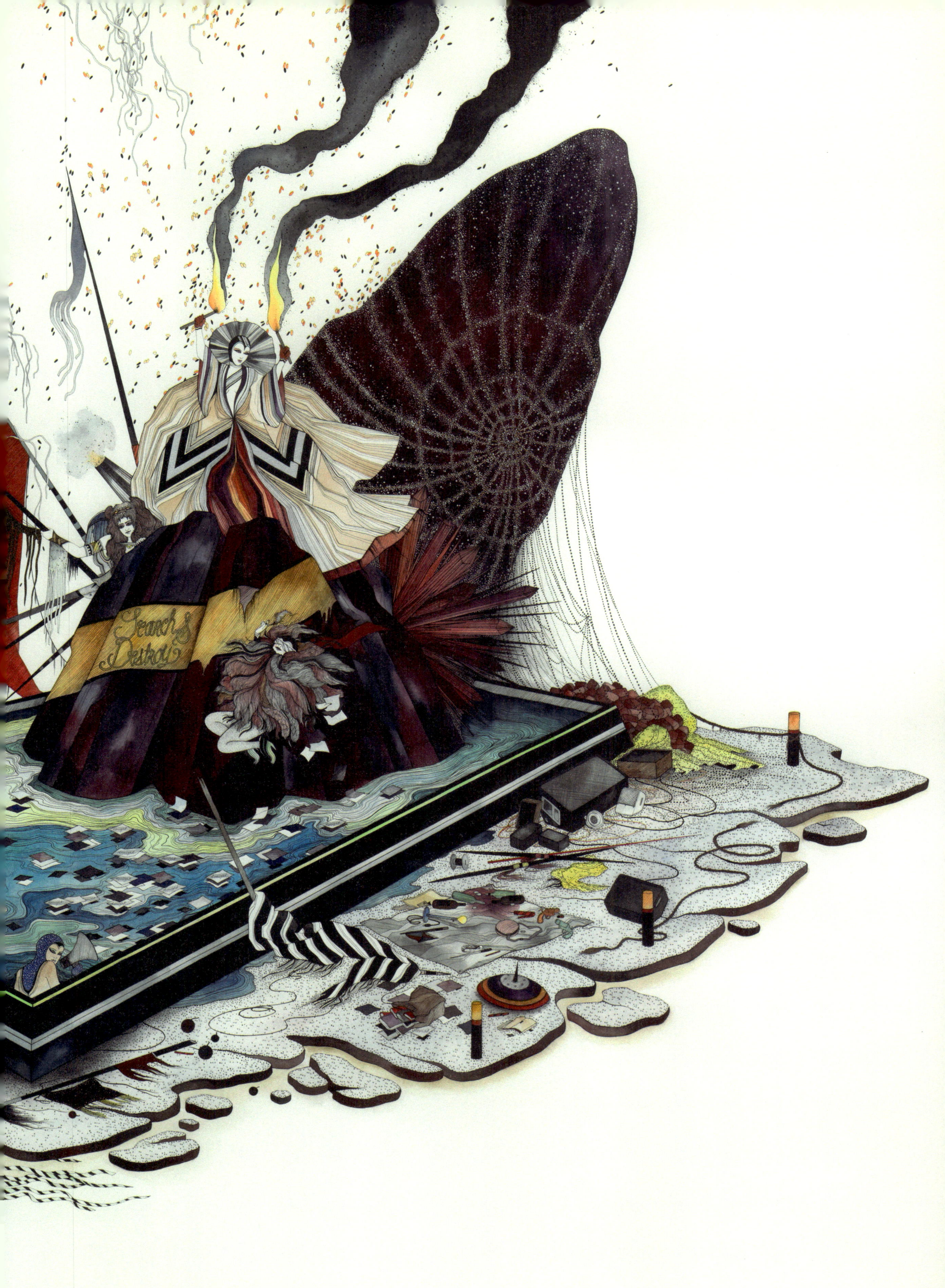
Search &
Destroy

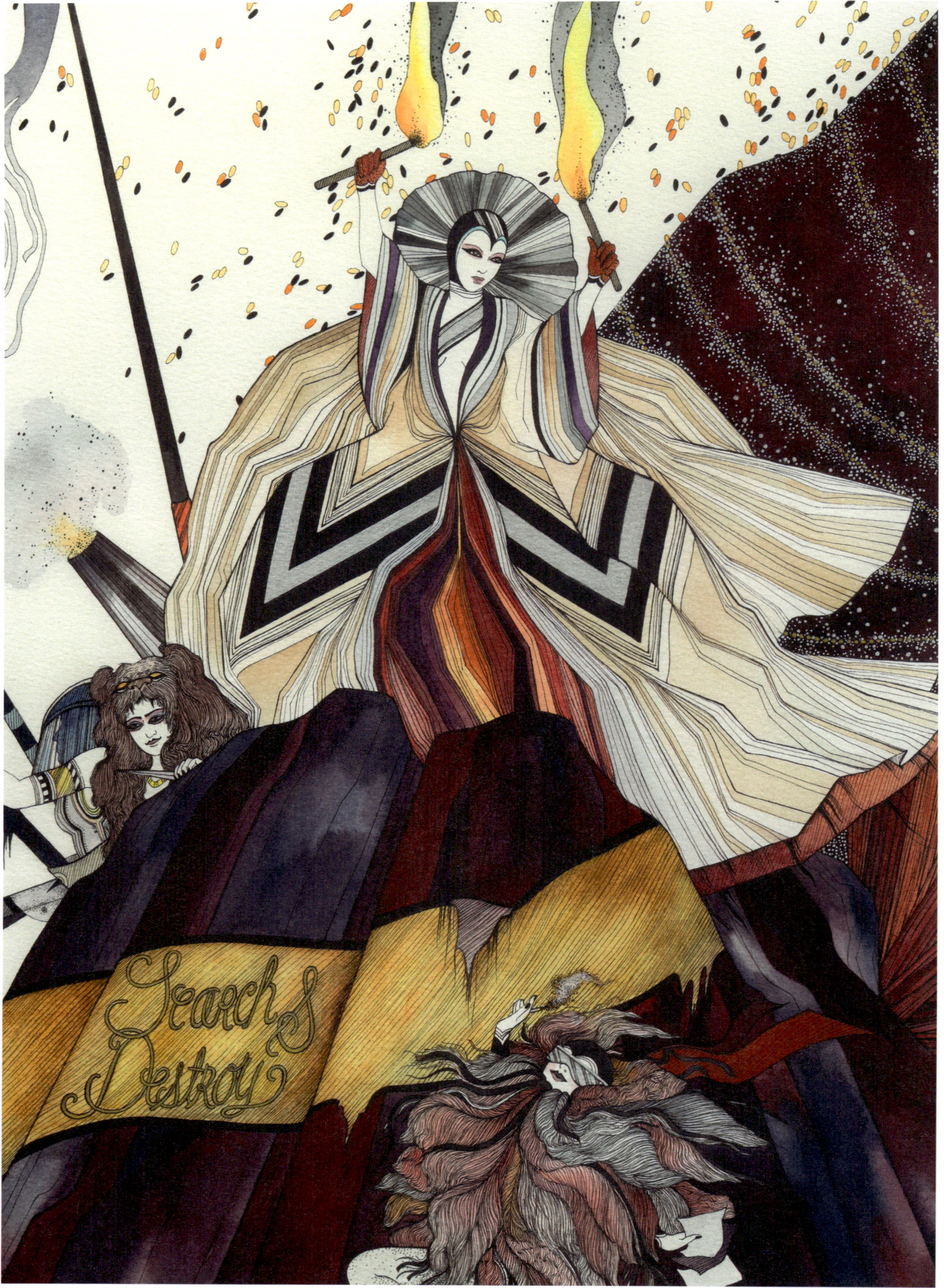
Search &
Destroy

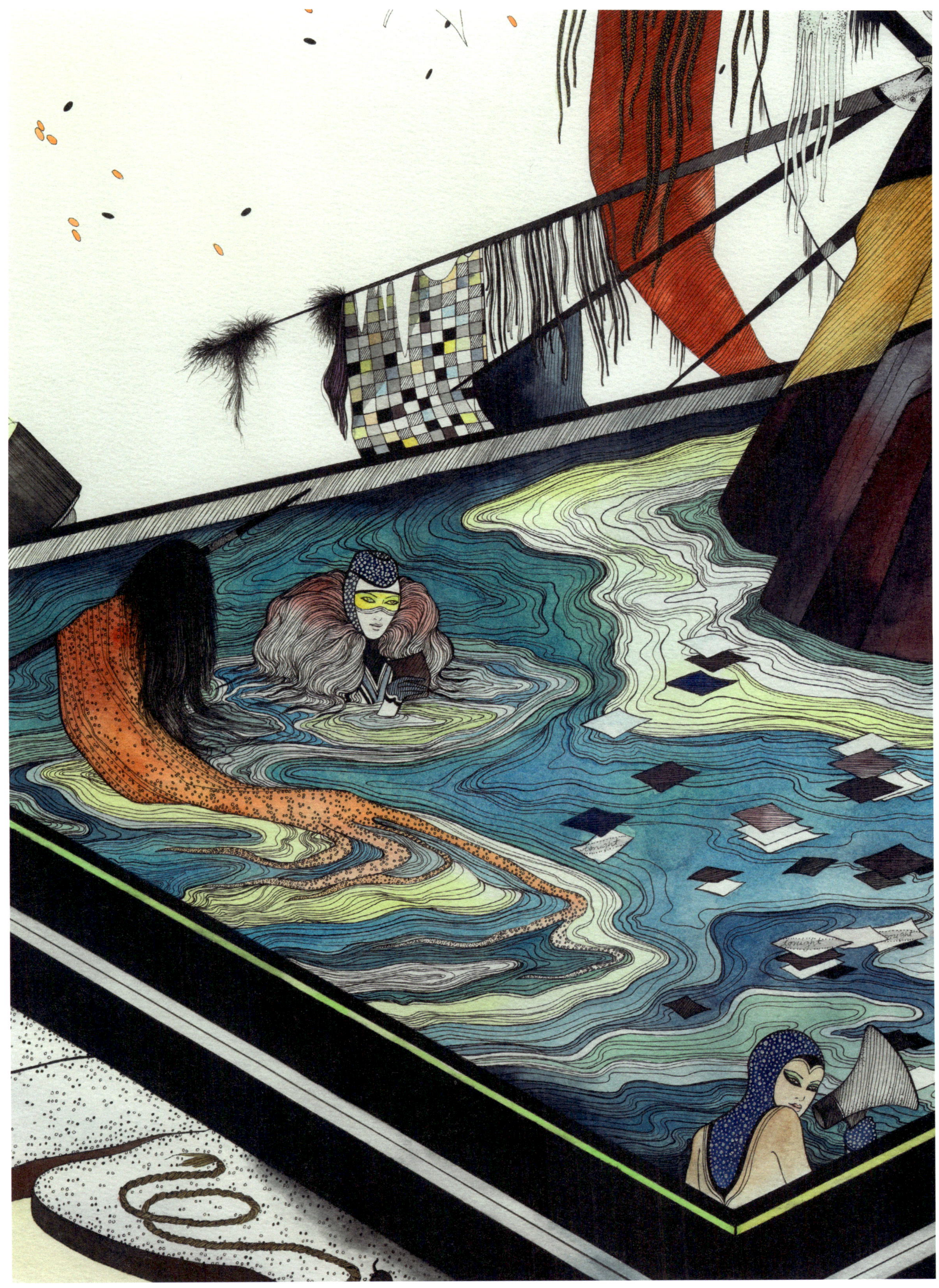
tonight
tonight

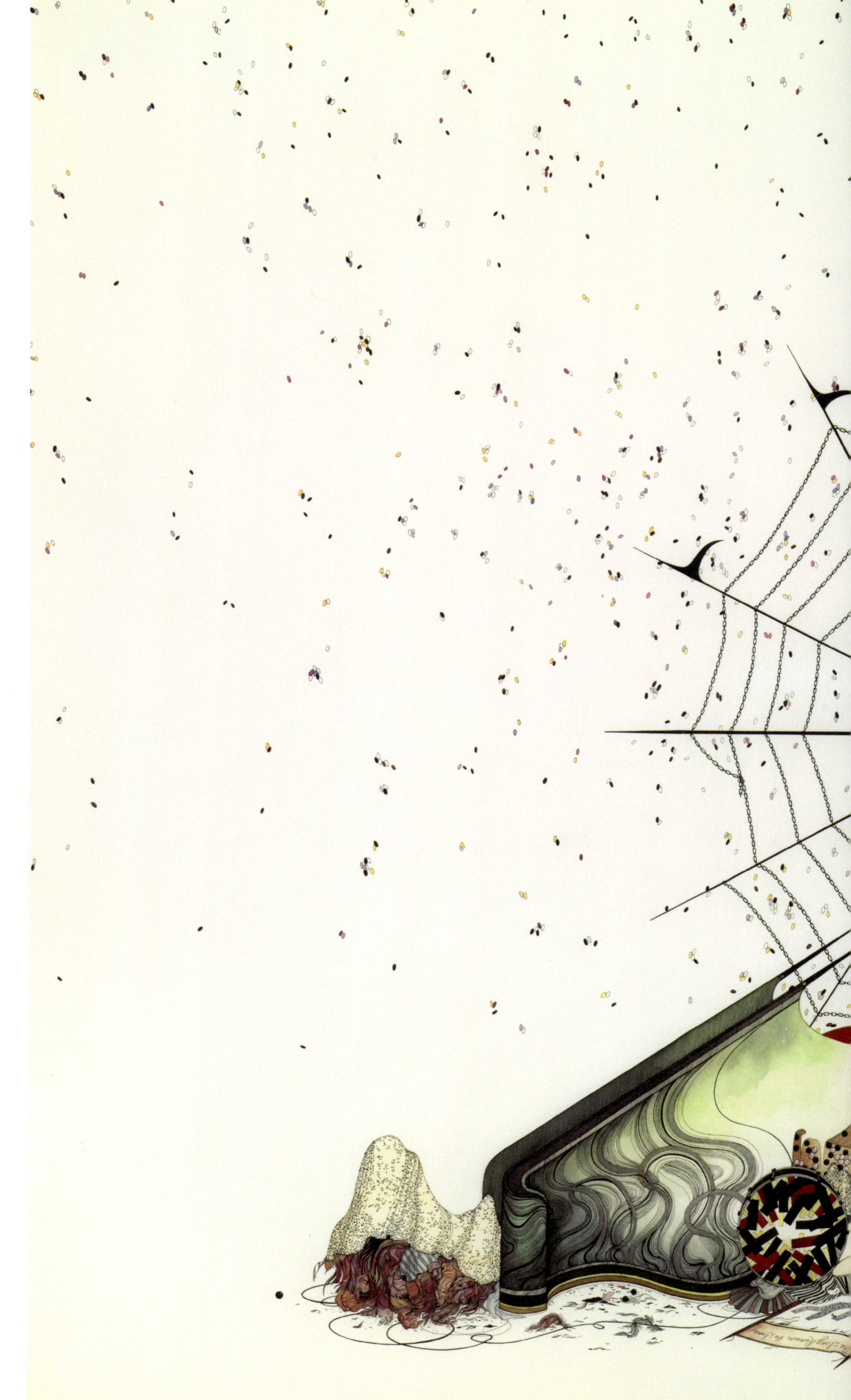

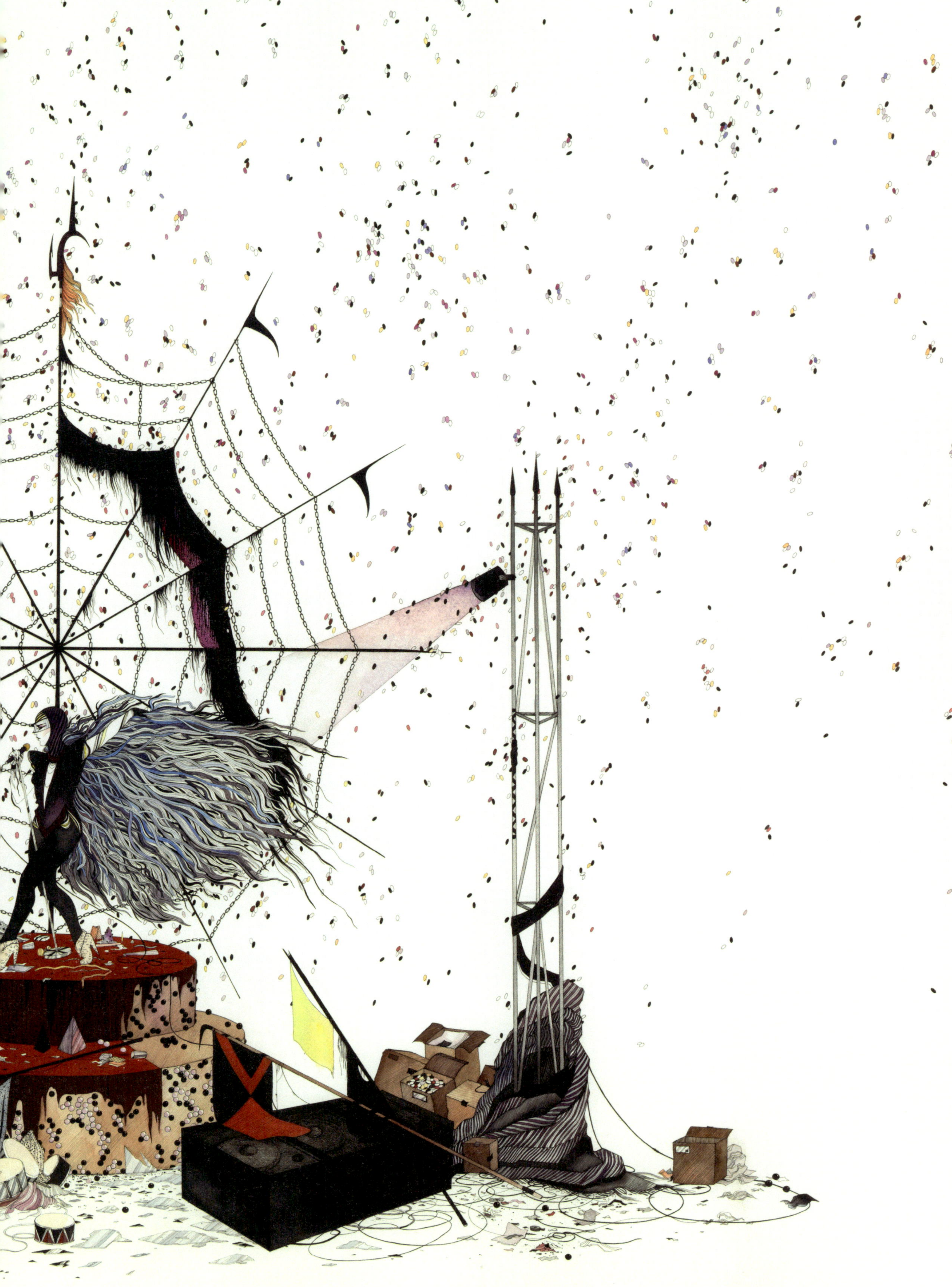

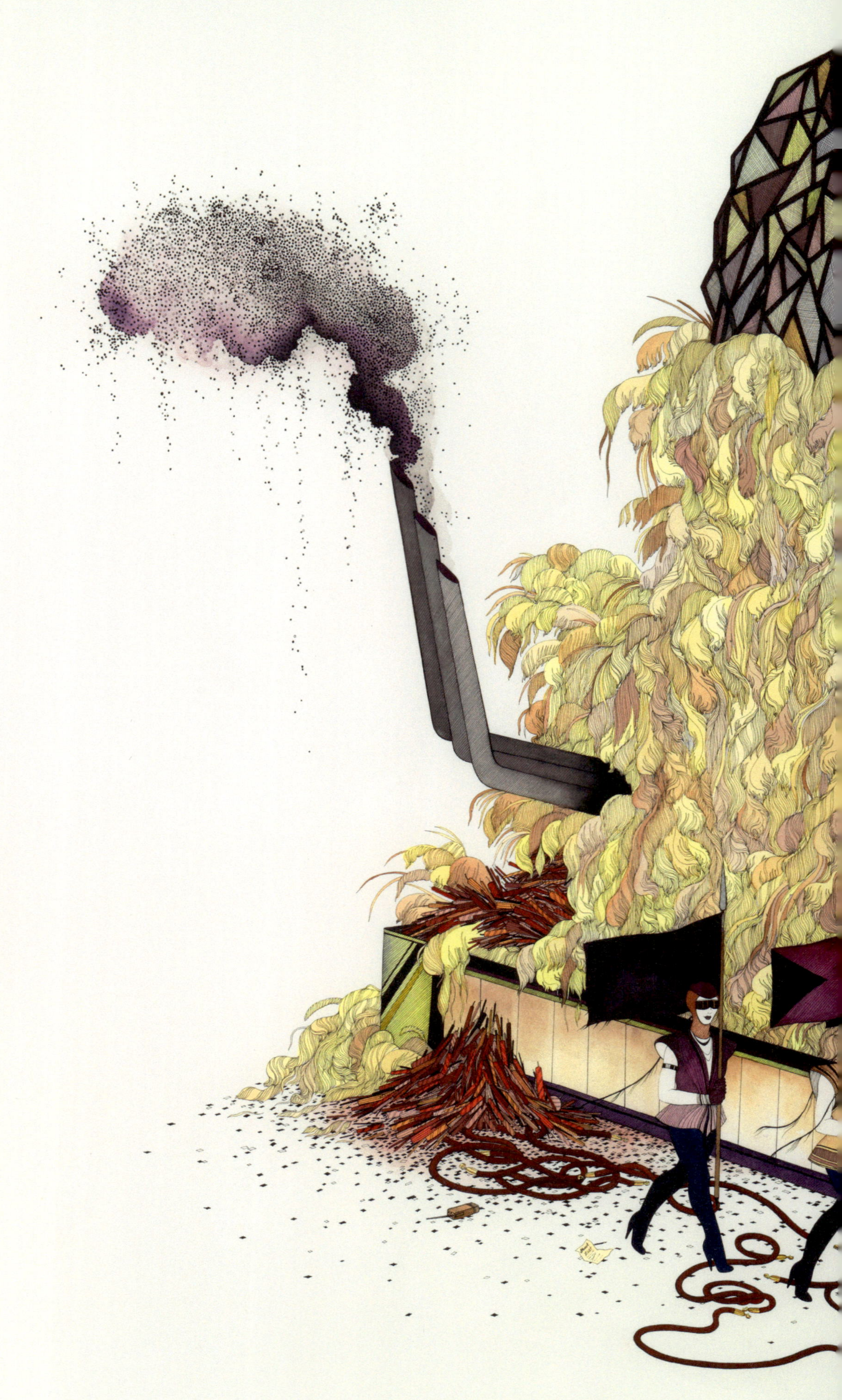

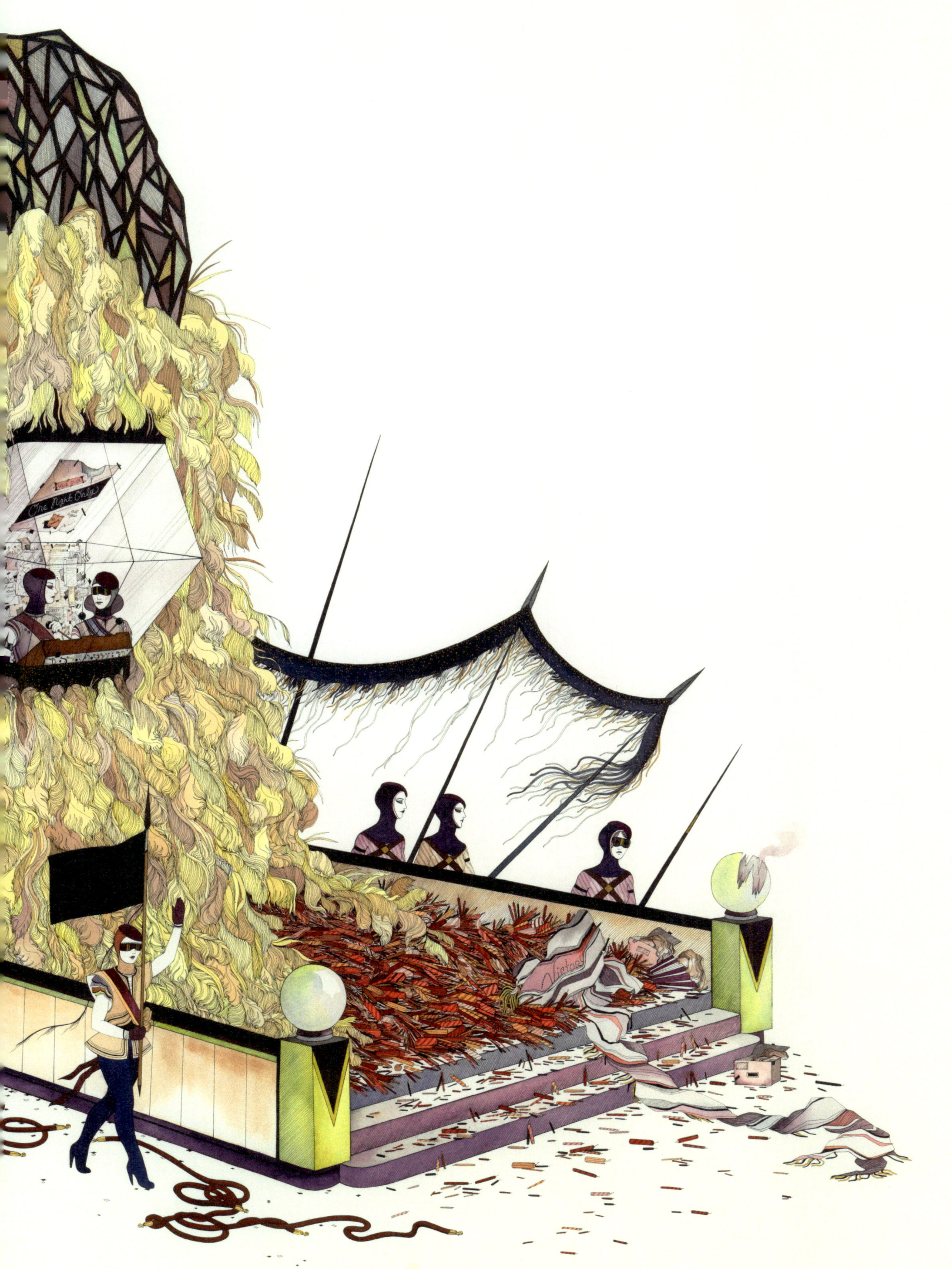
HELD OVER
One Night Only
Victory

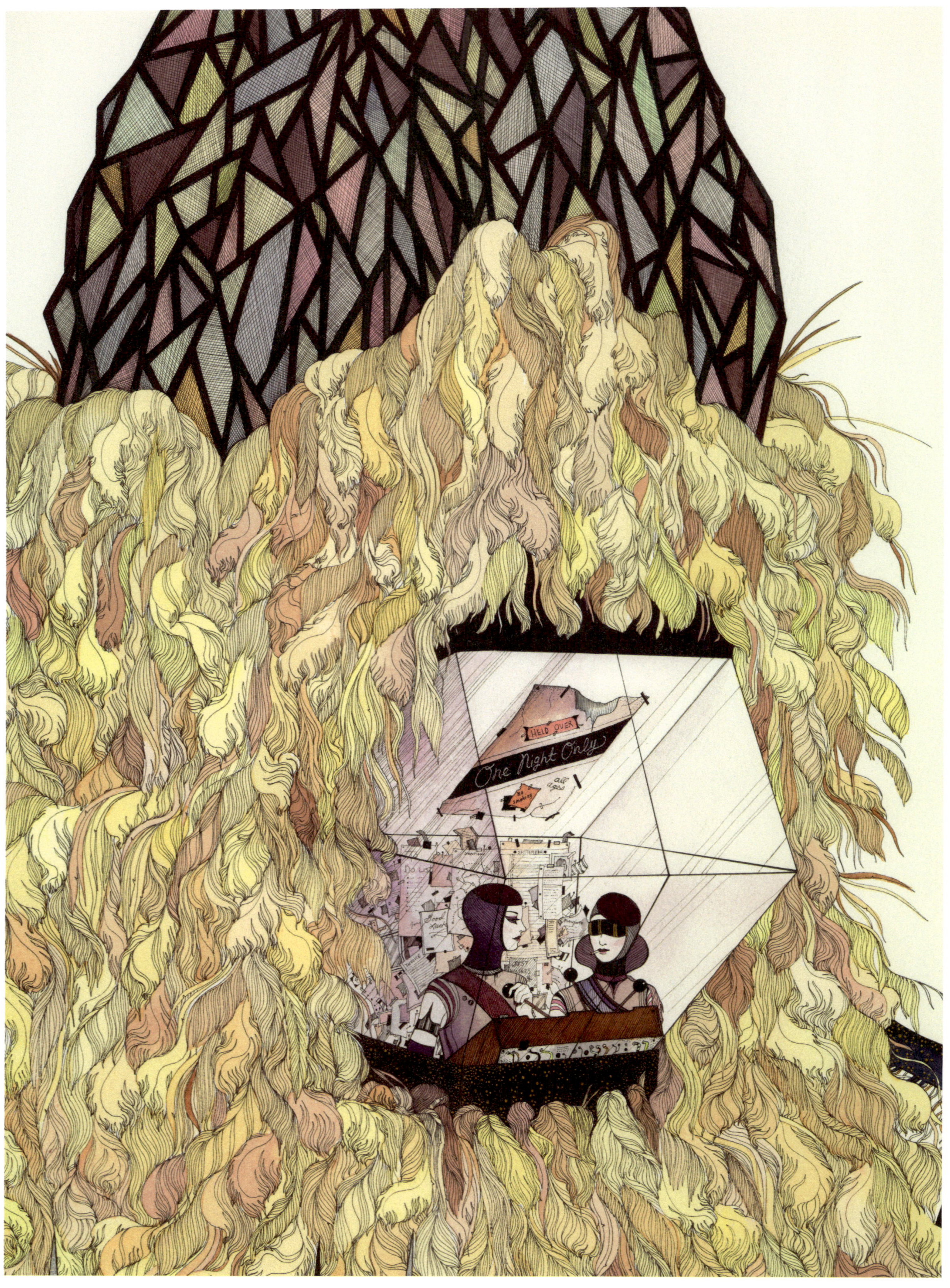
HELD OVER
One Night Only
all ages
No smoking

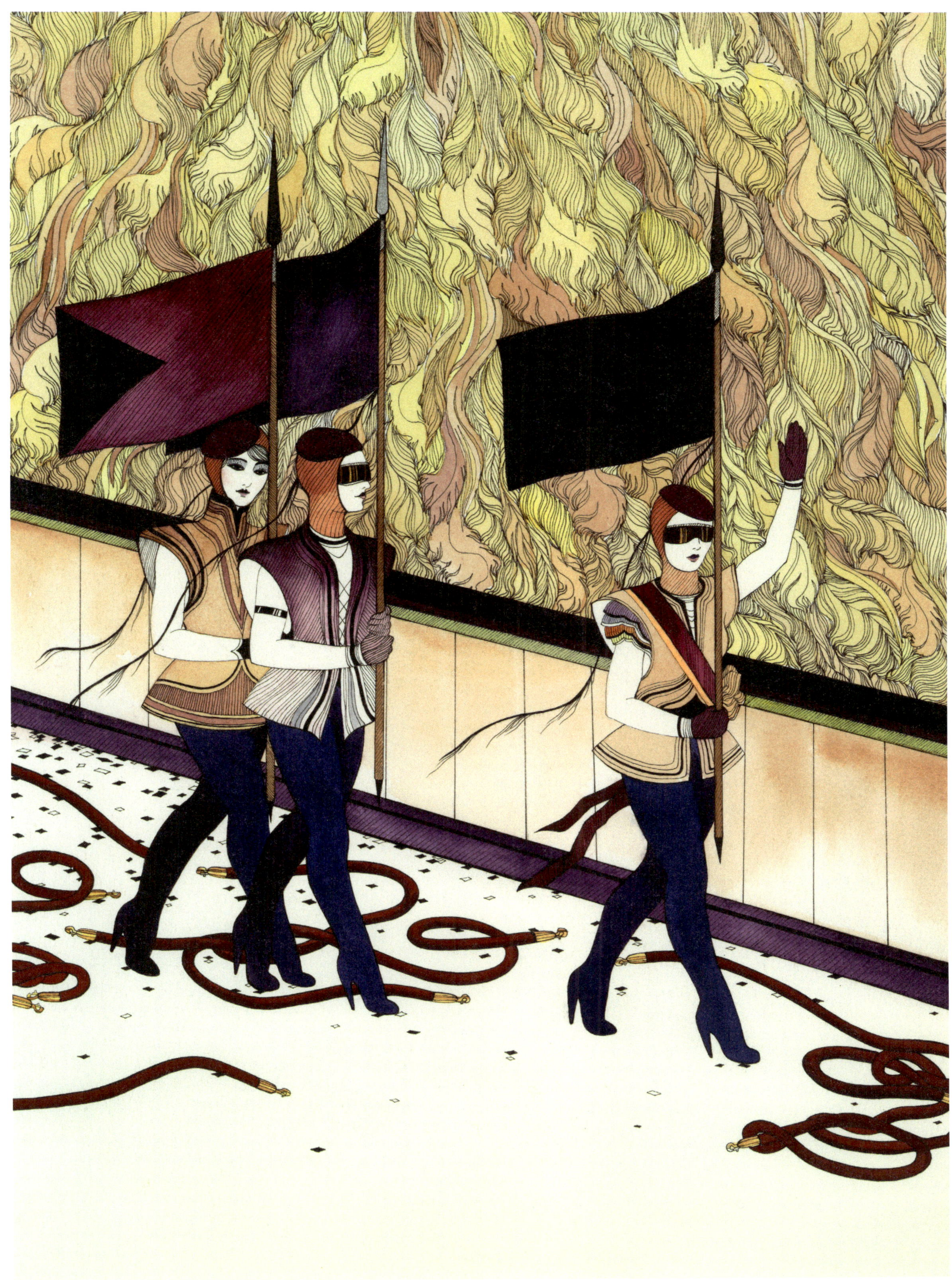

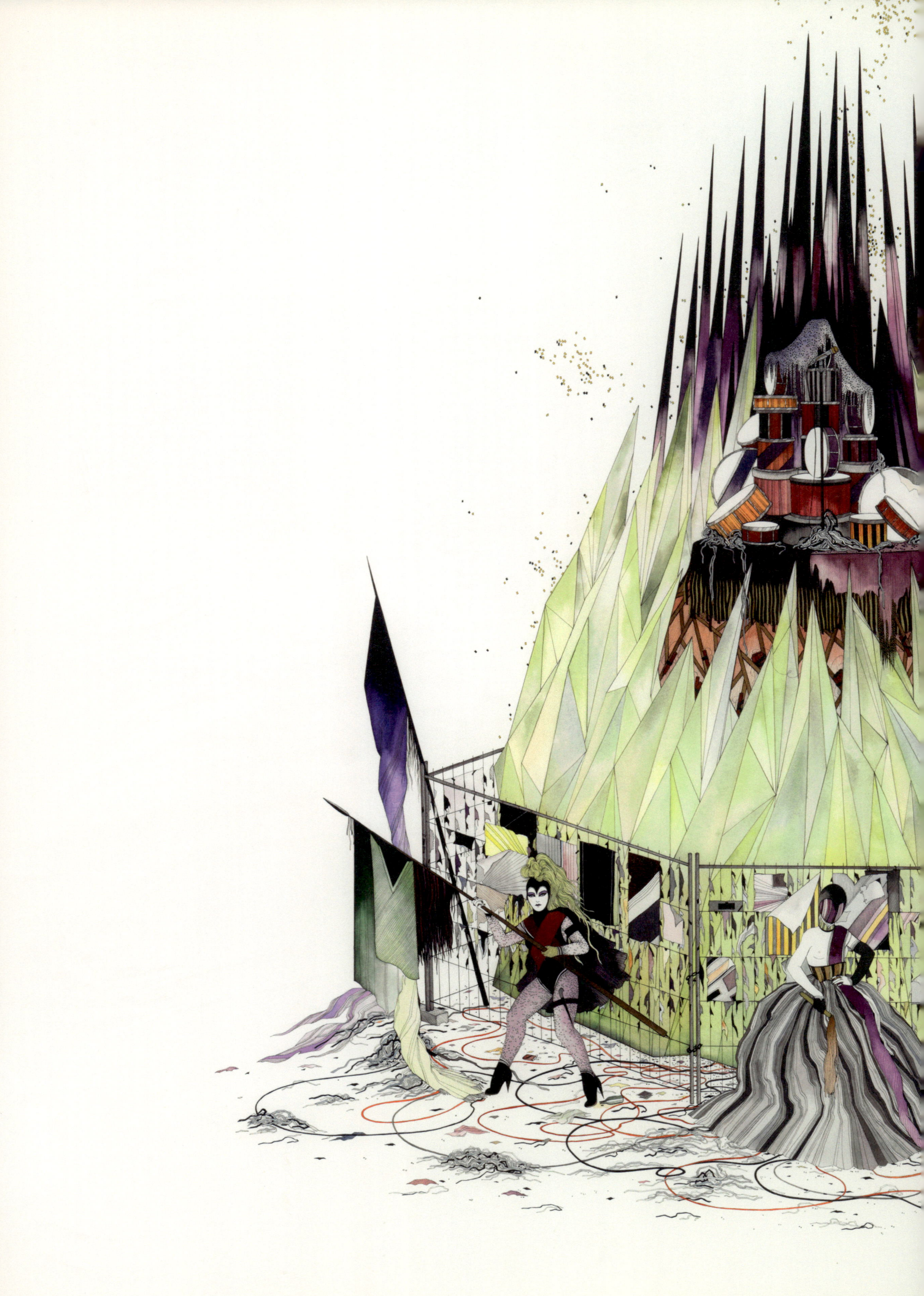

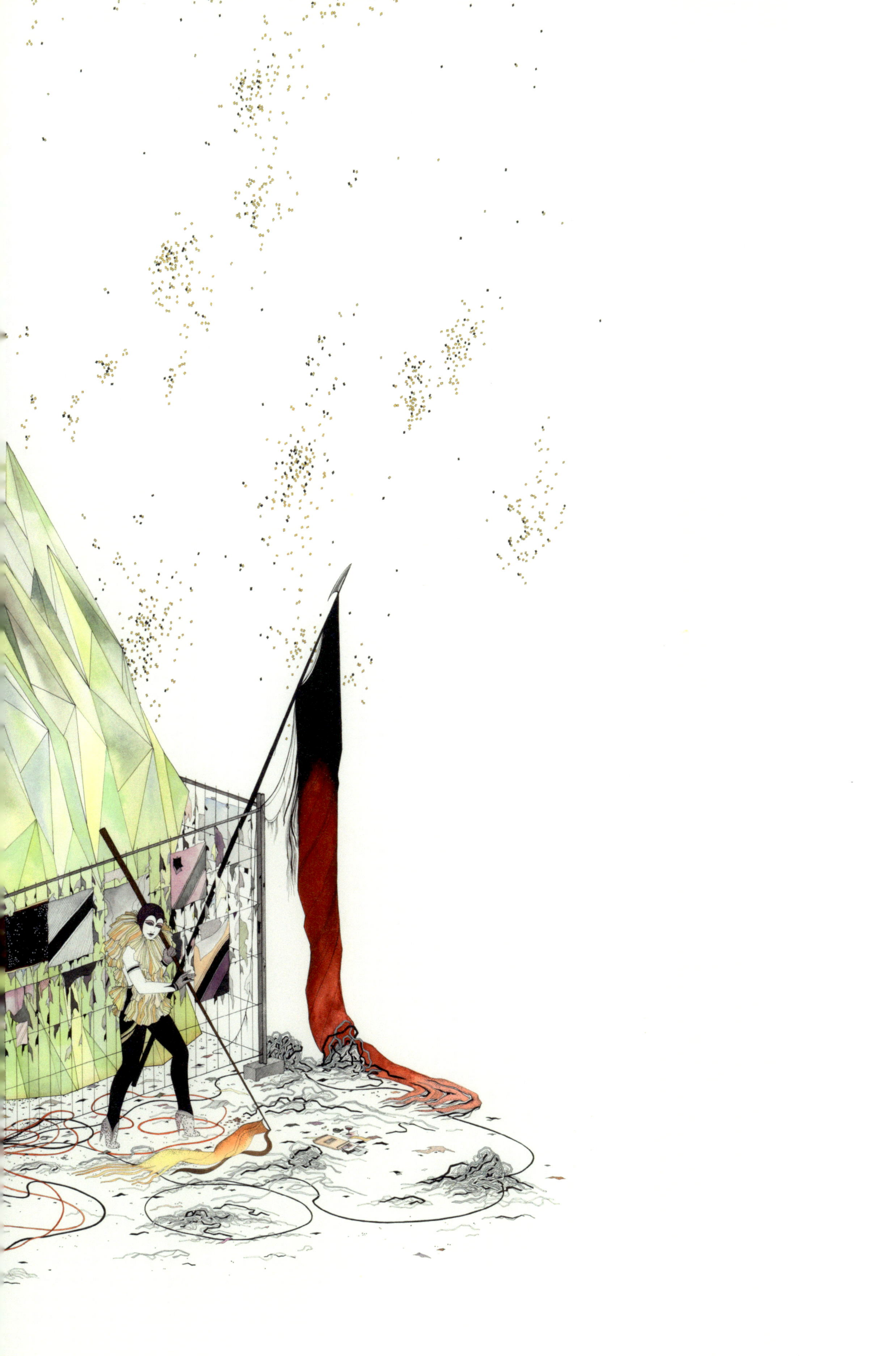

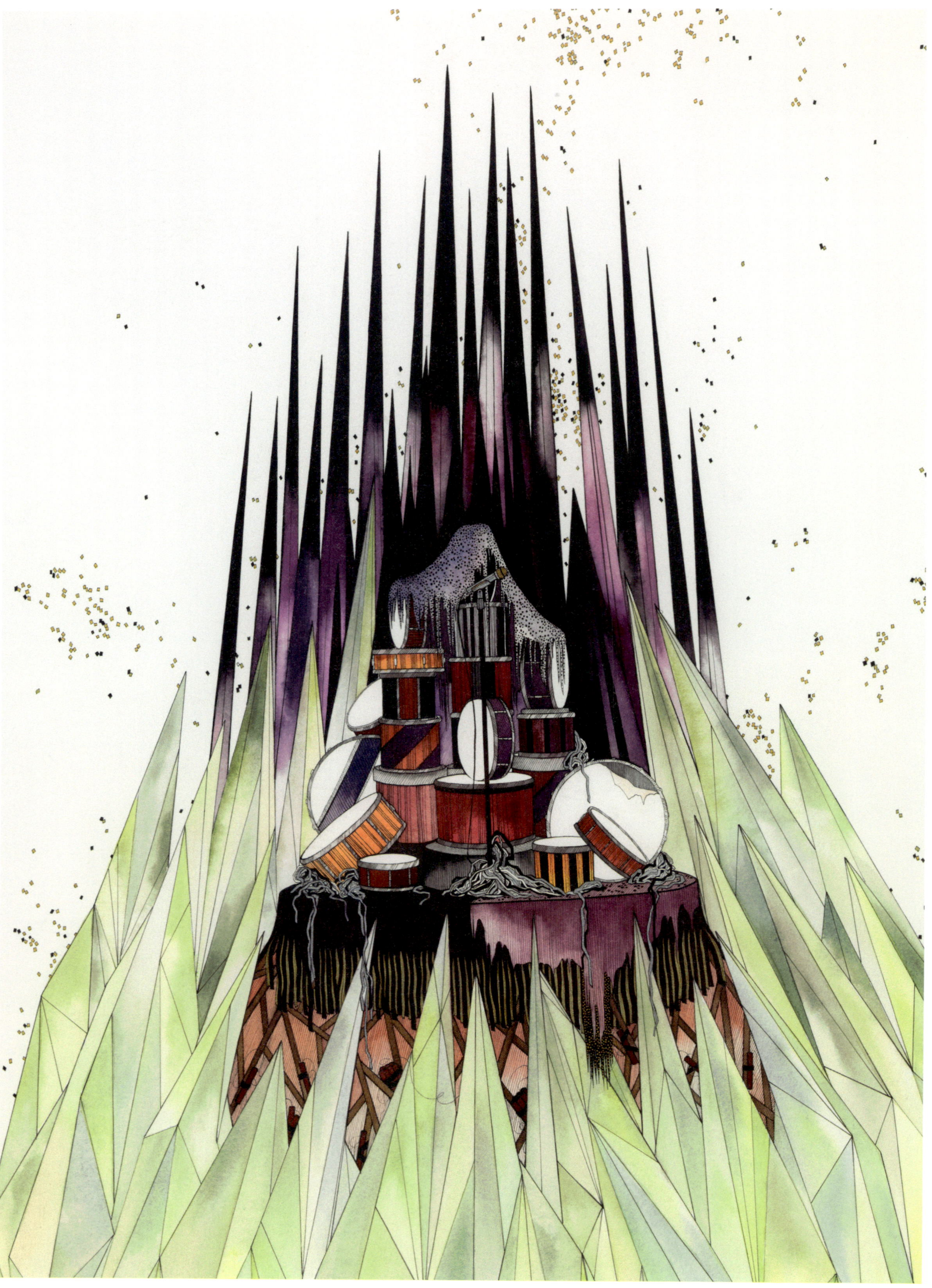

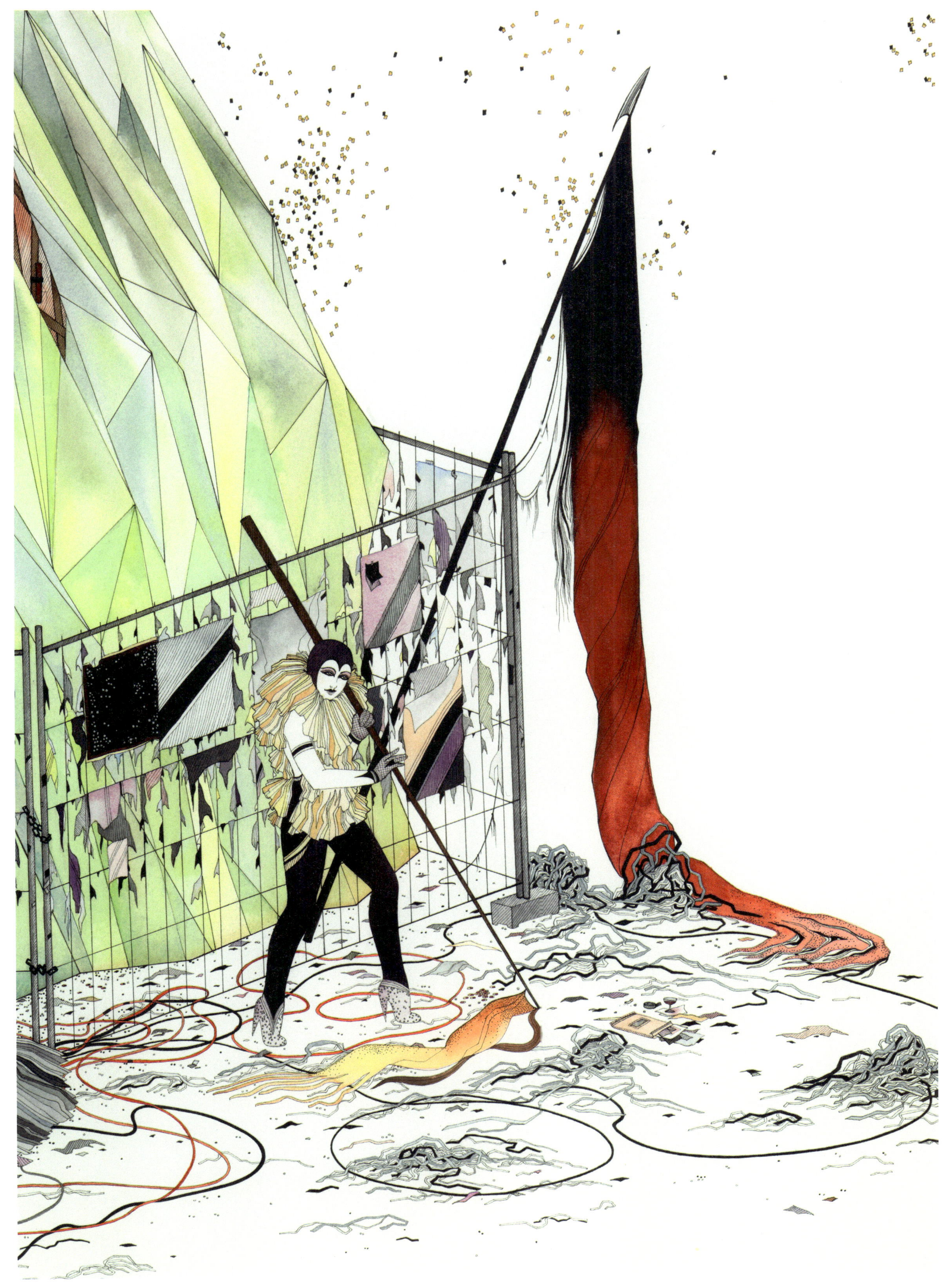

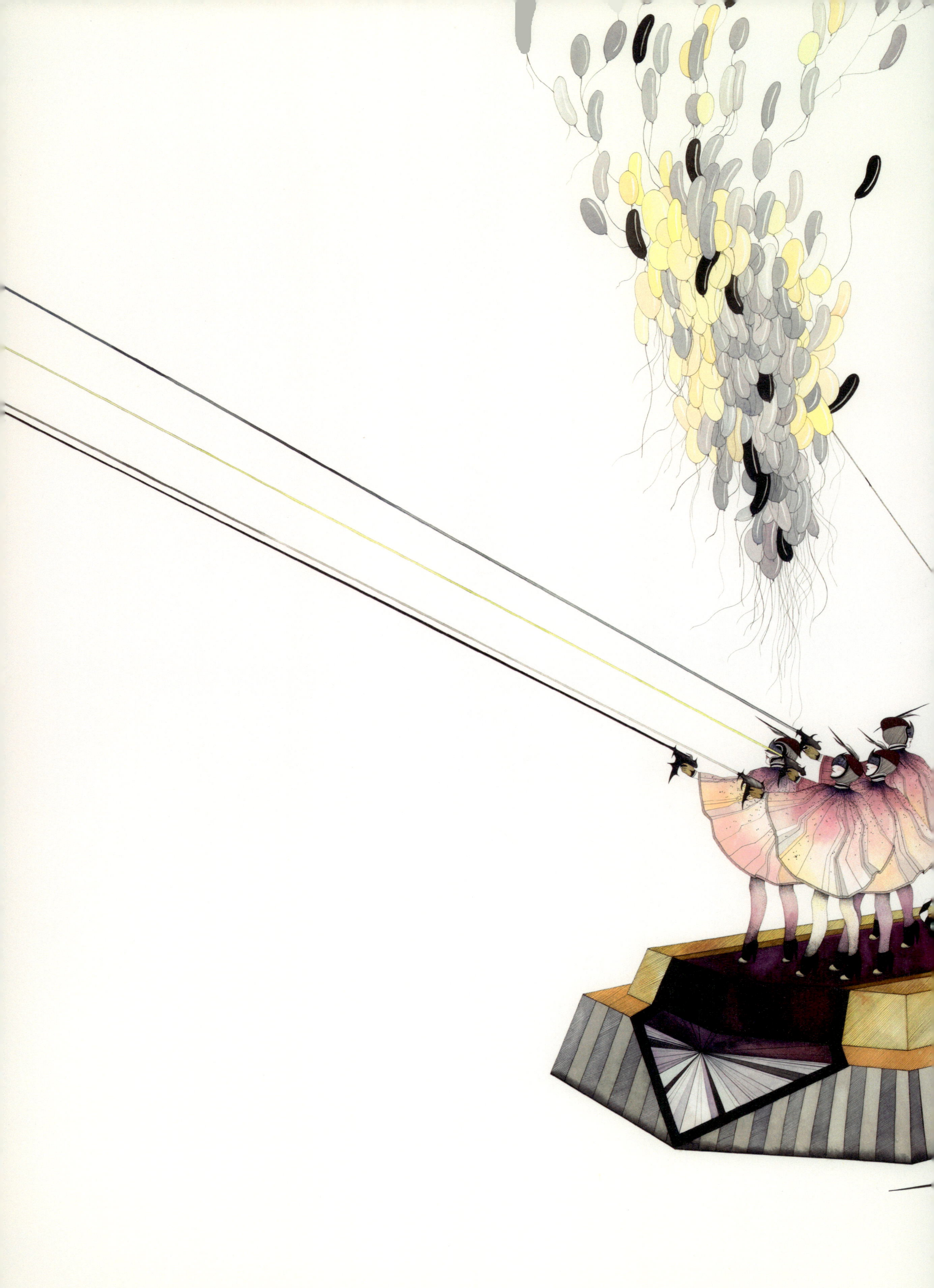

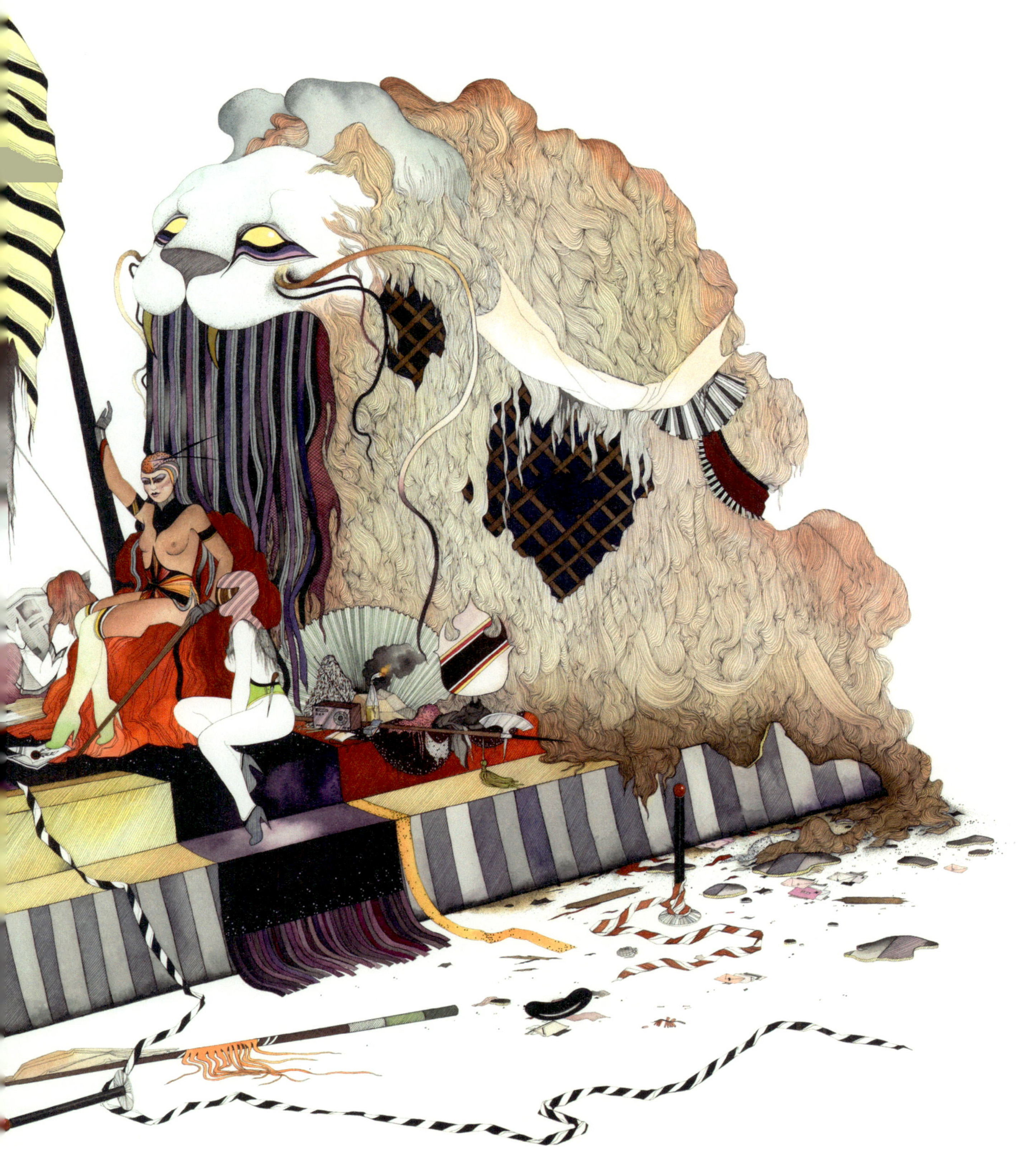

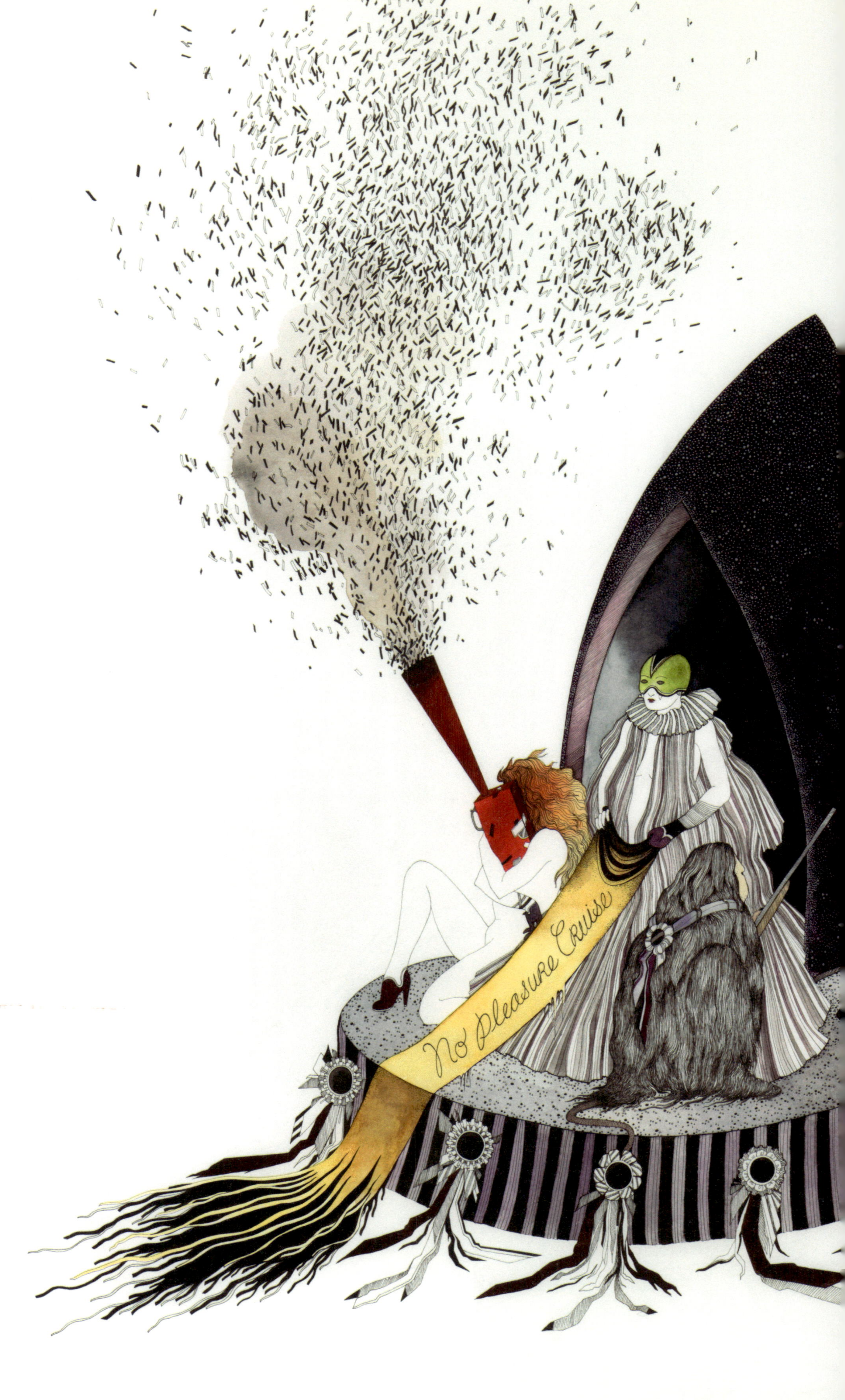
No pleasure Cruise

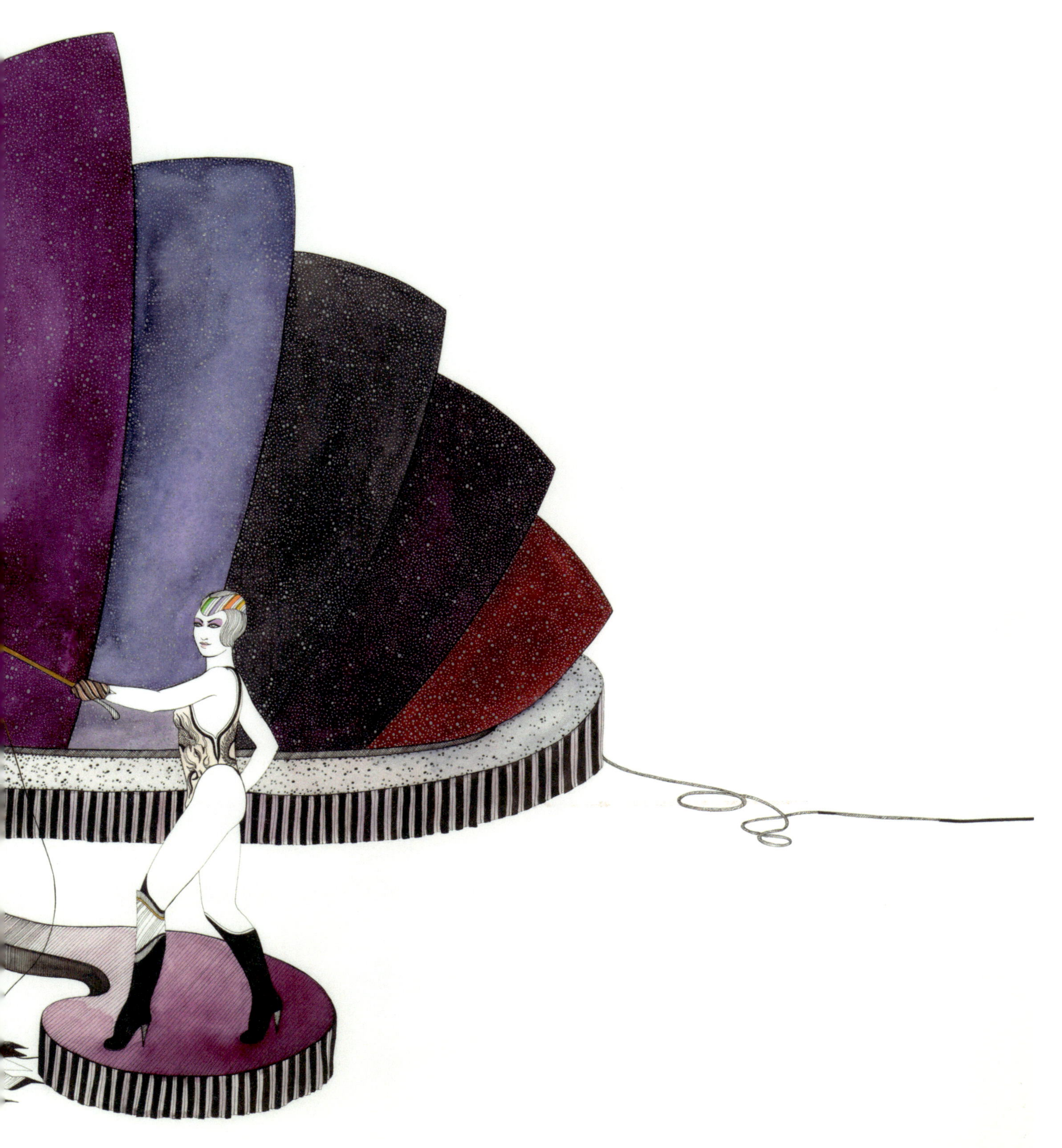

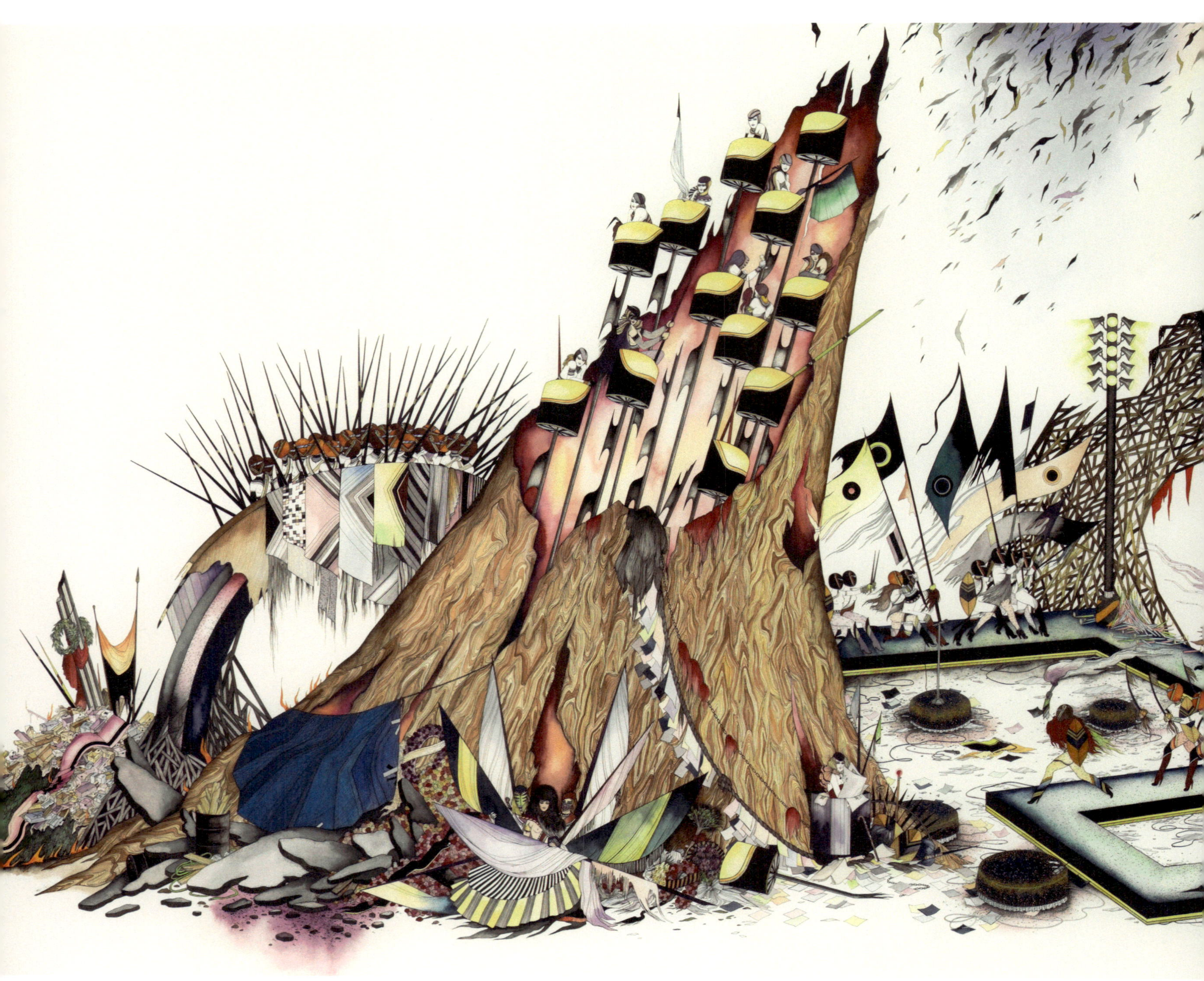

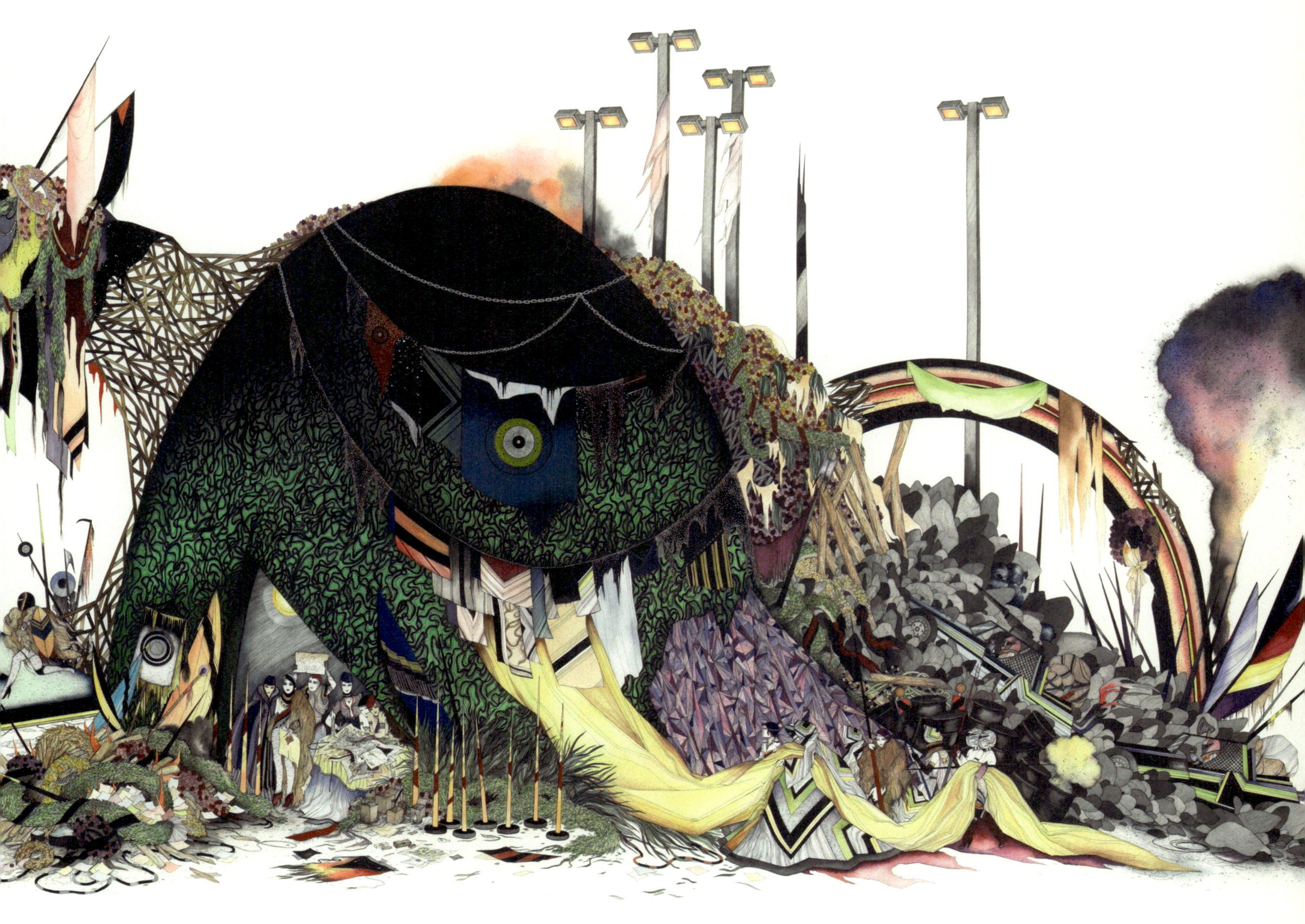

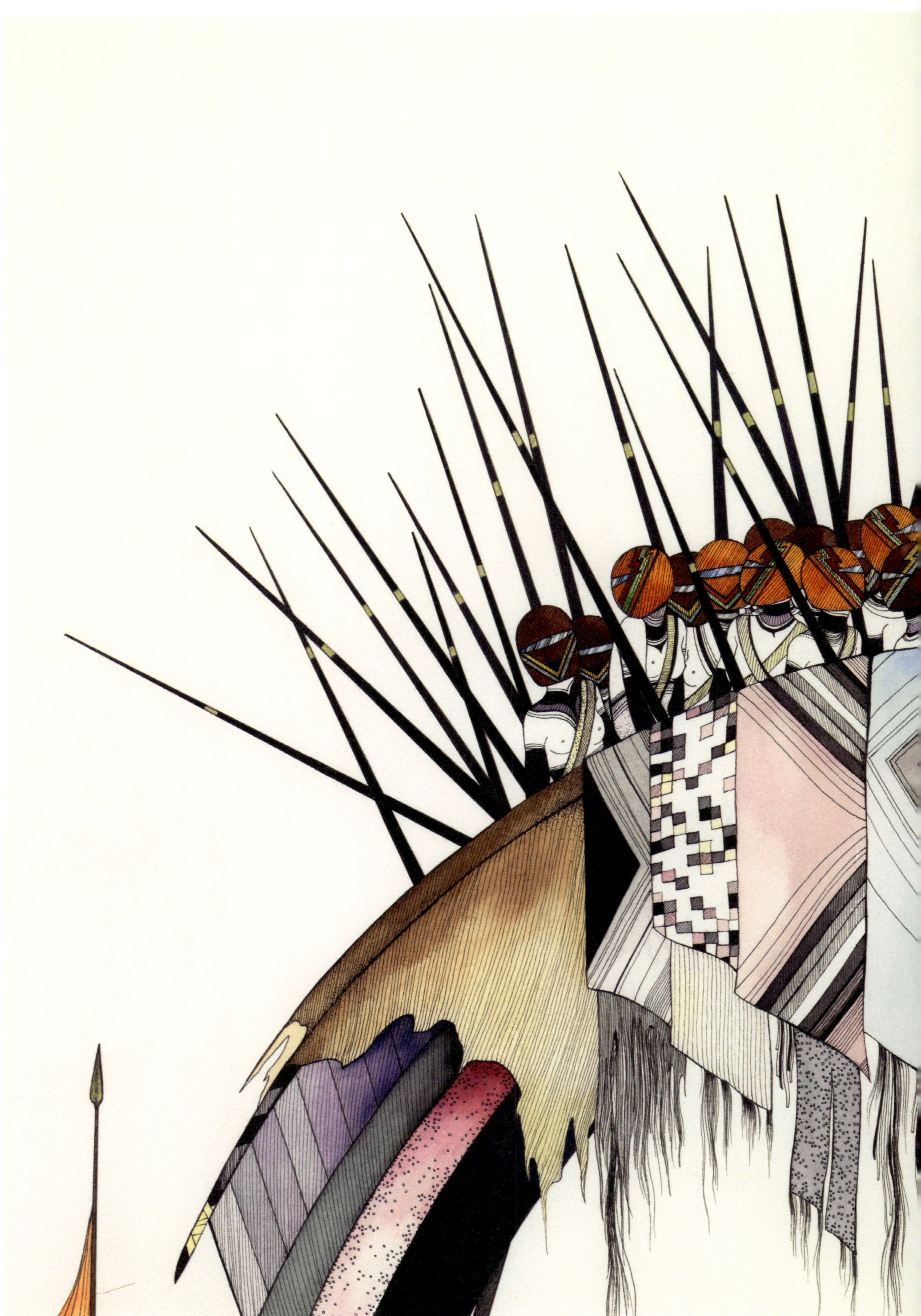

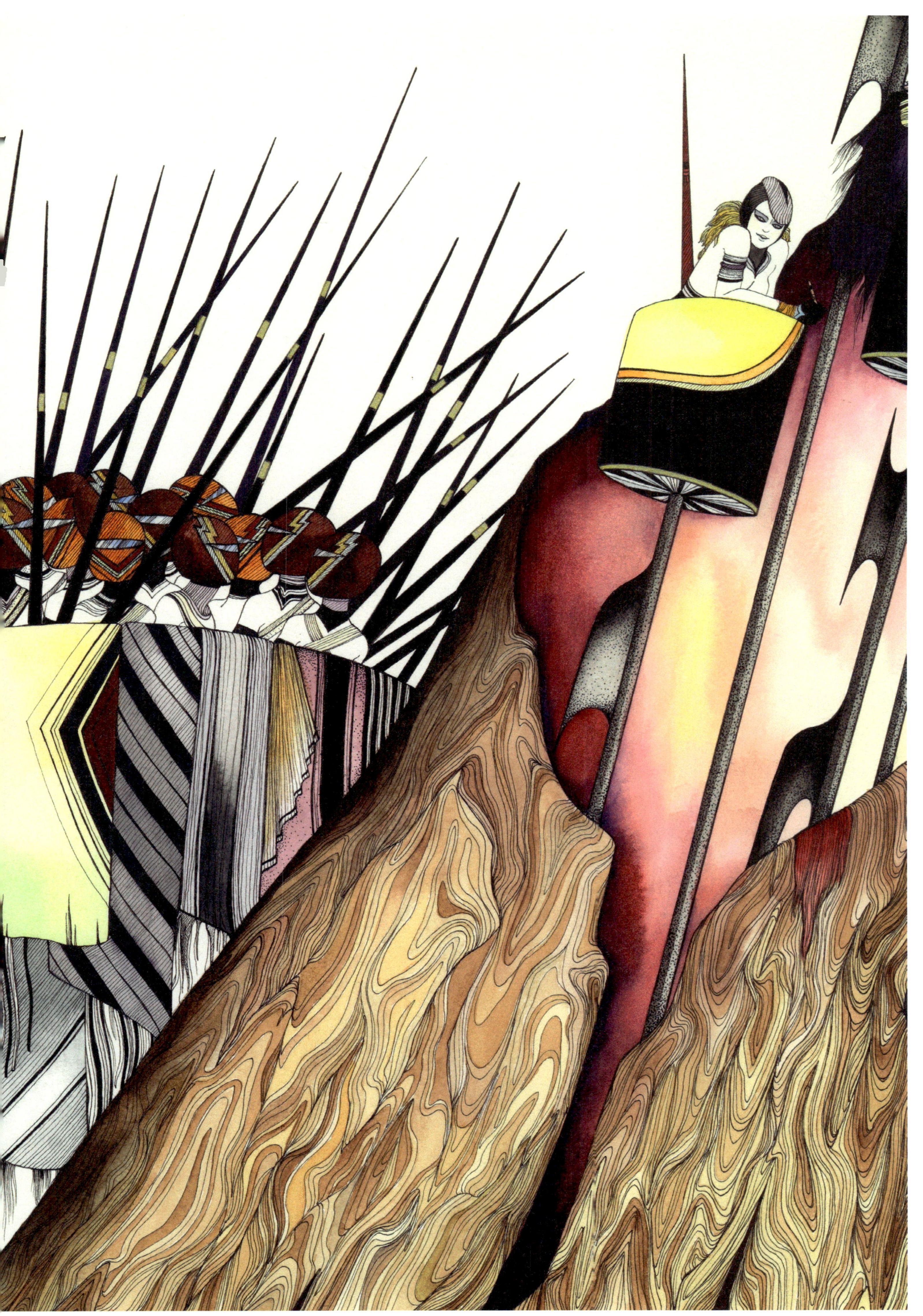

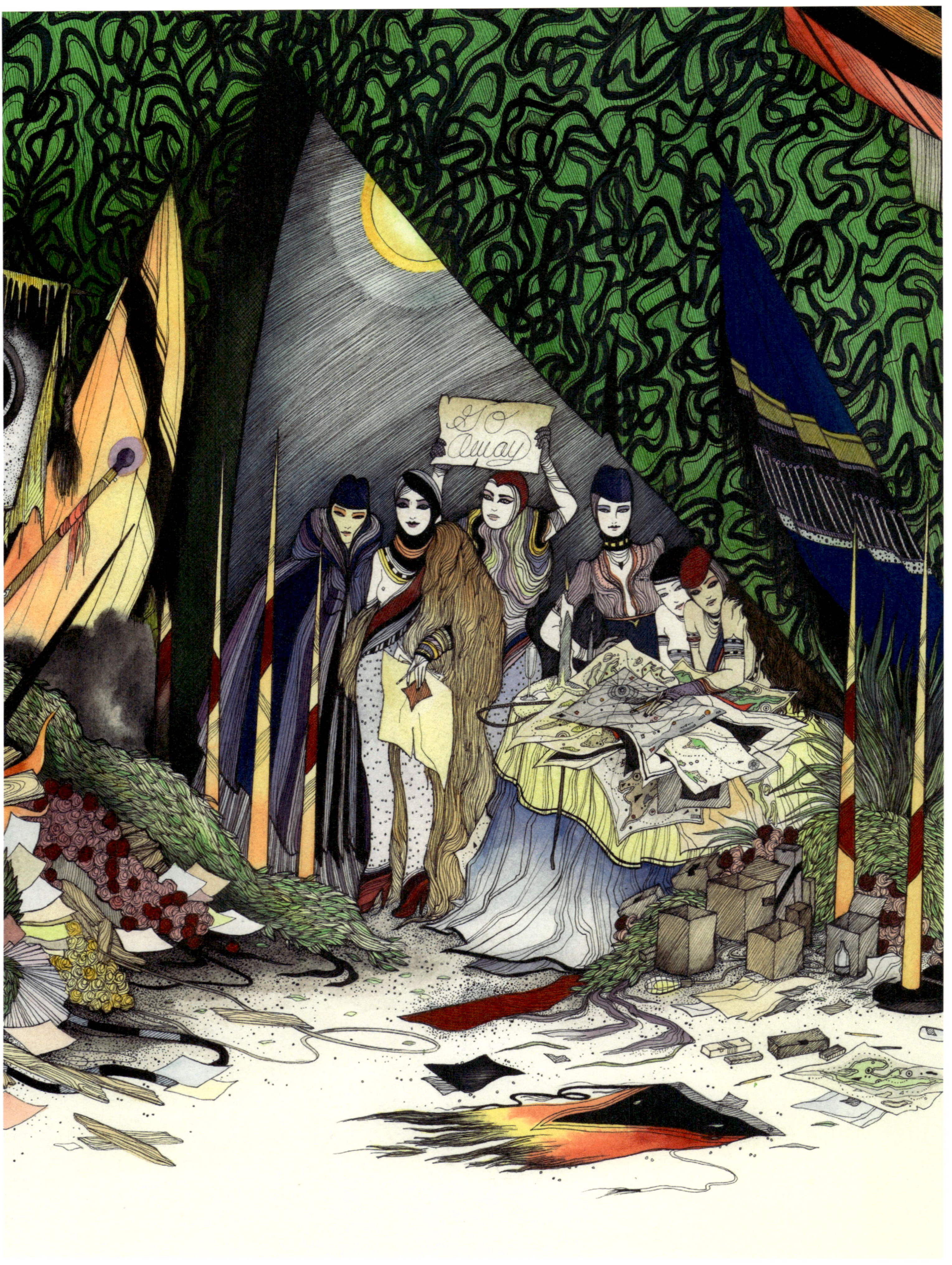
Go away

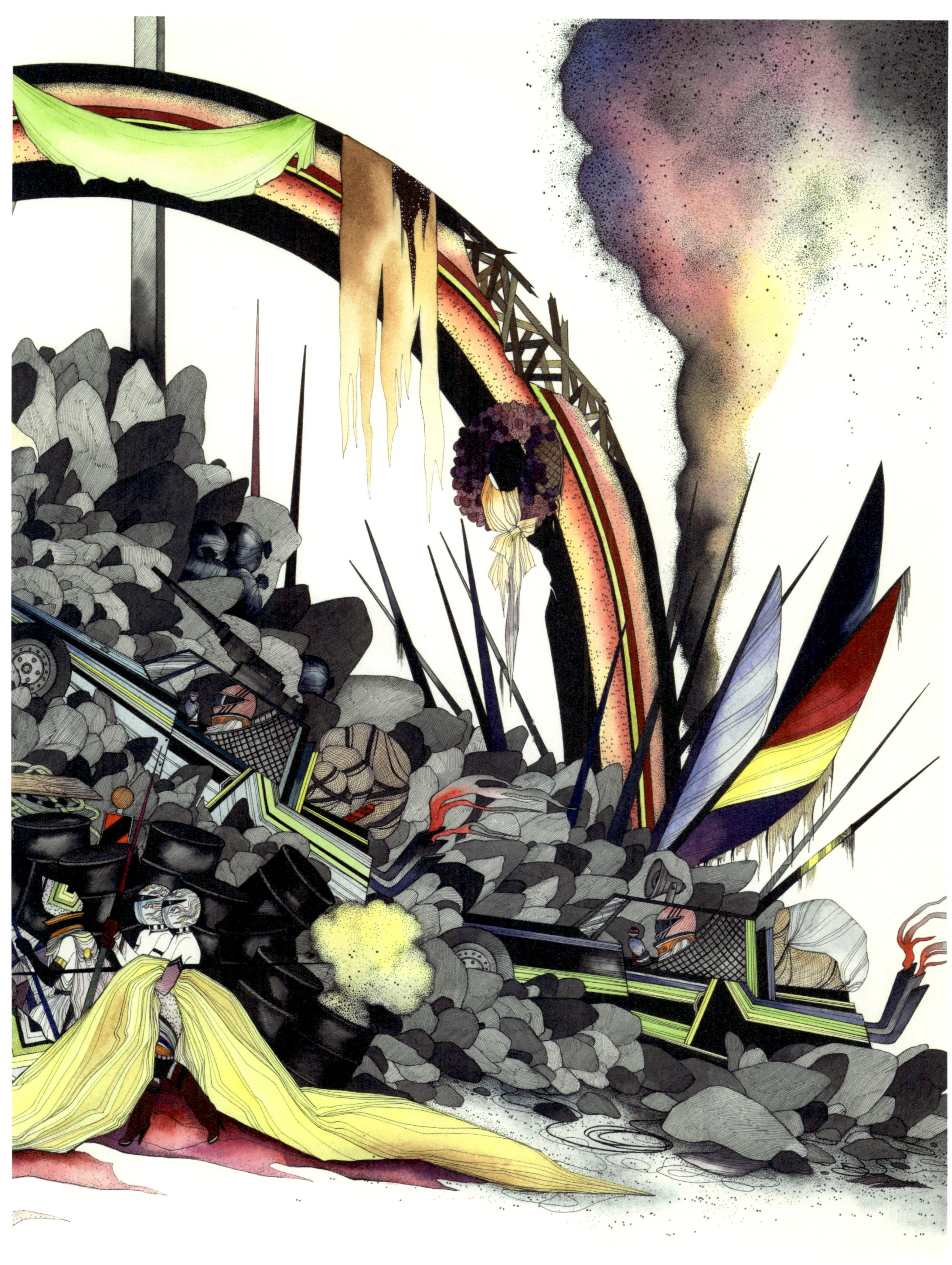

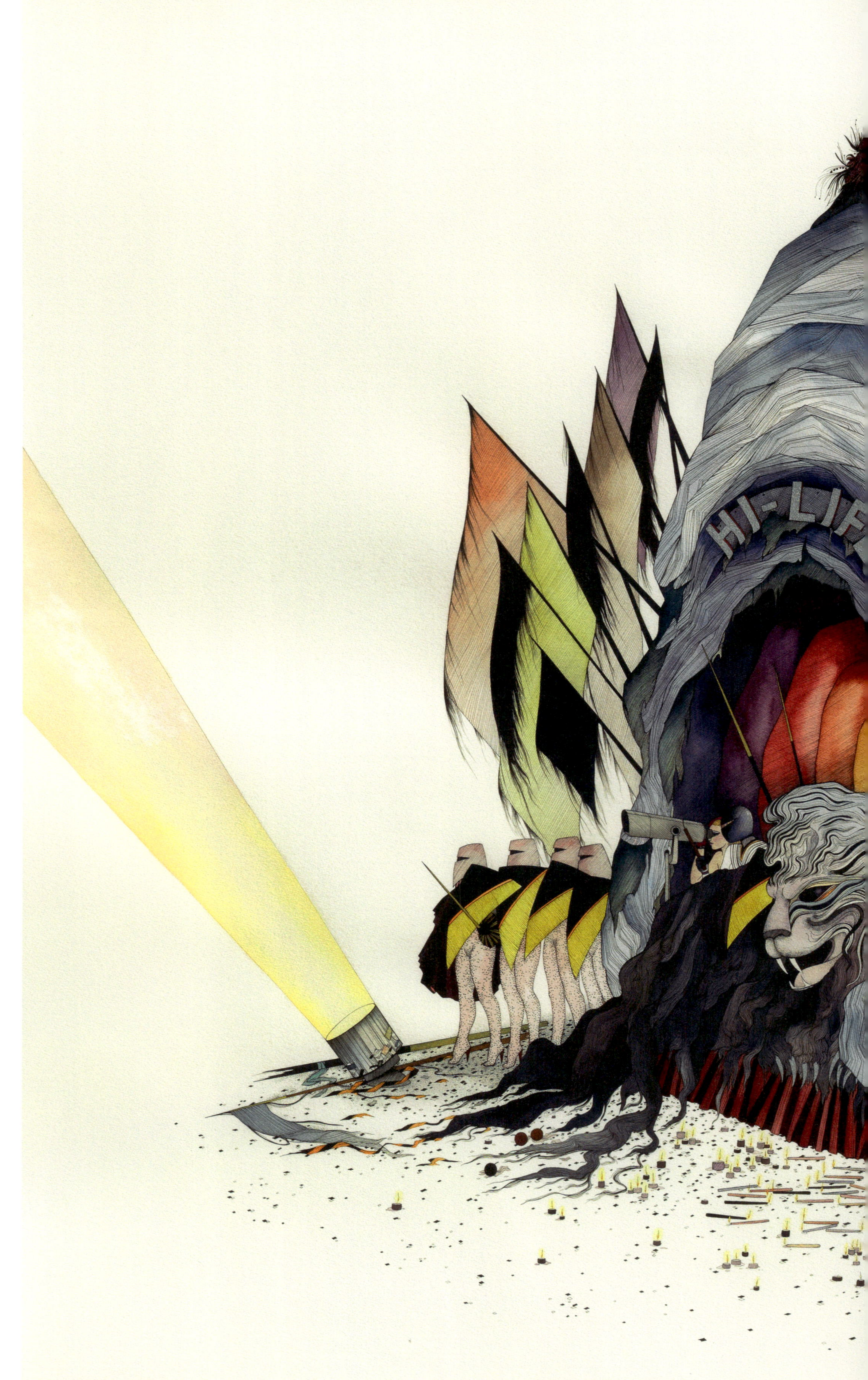

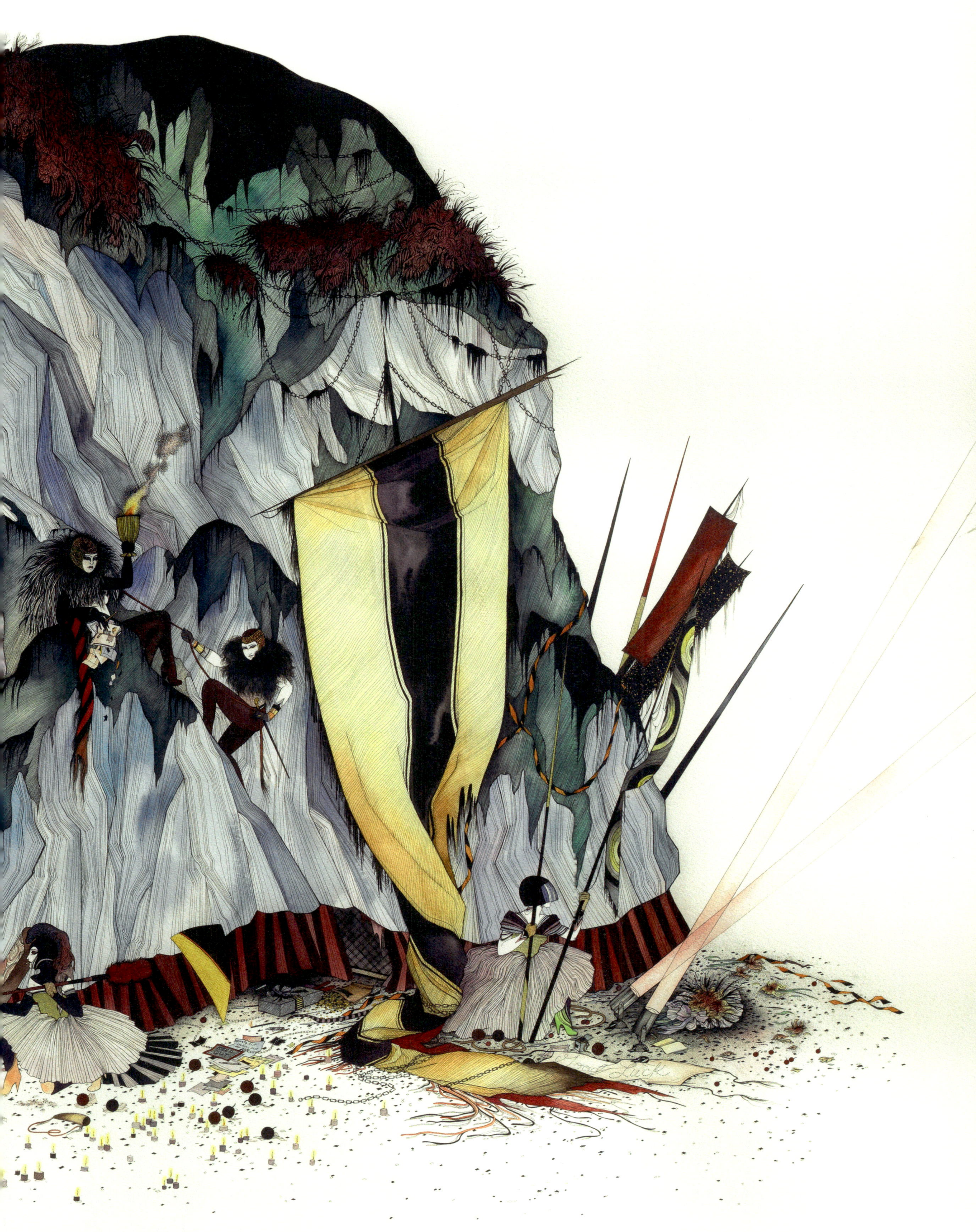
Good Luck

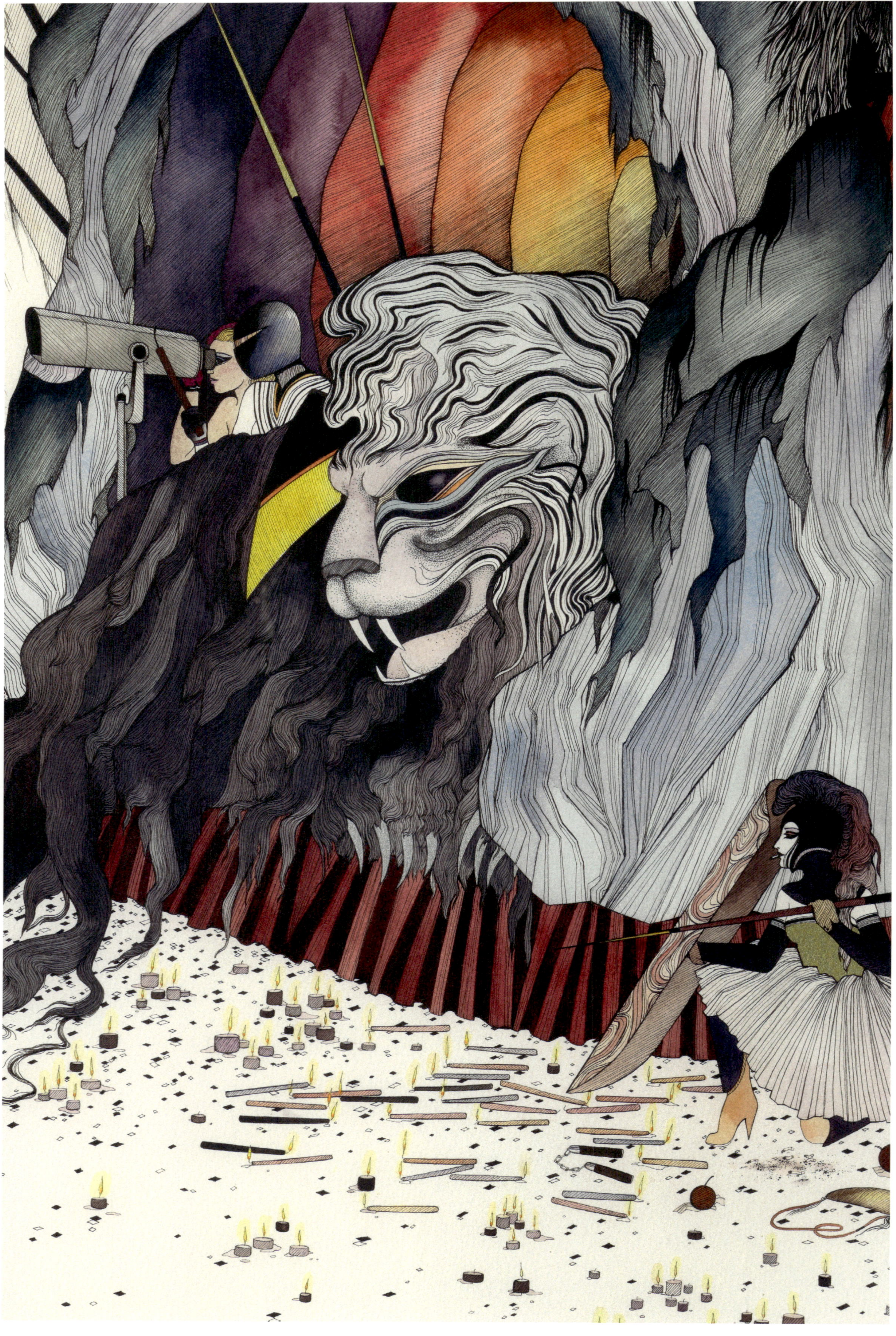

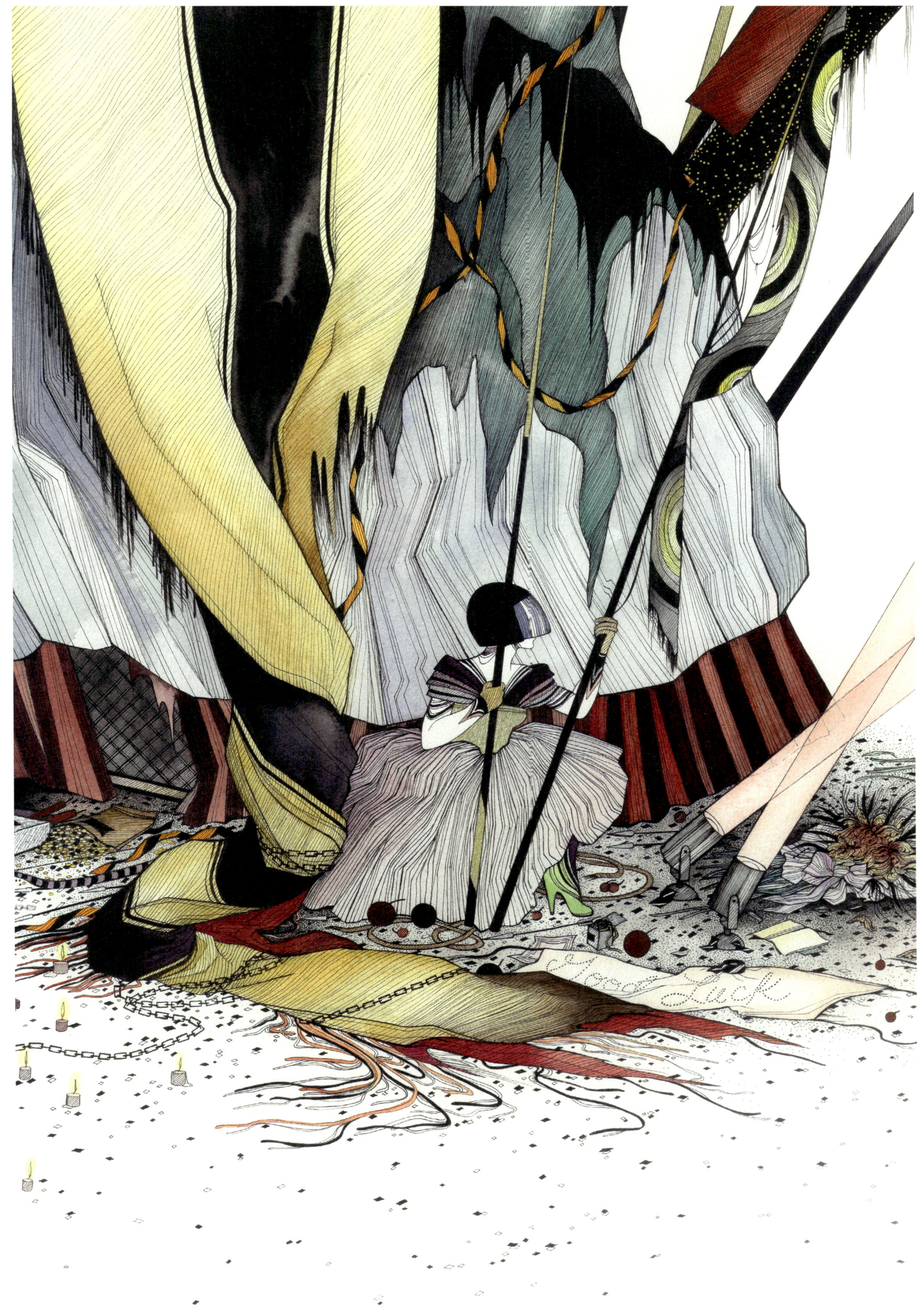
Good Luck

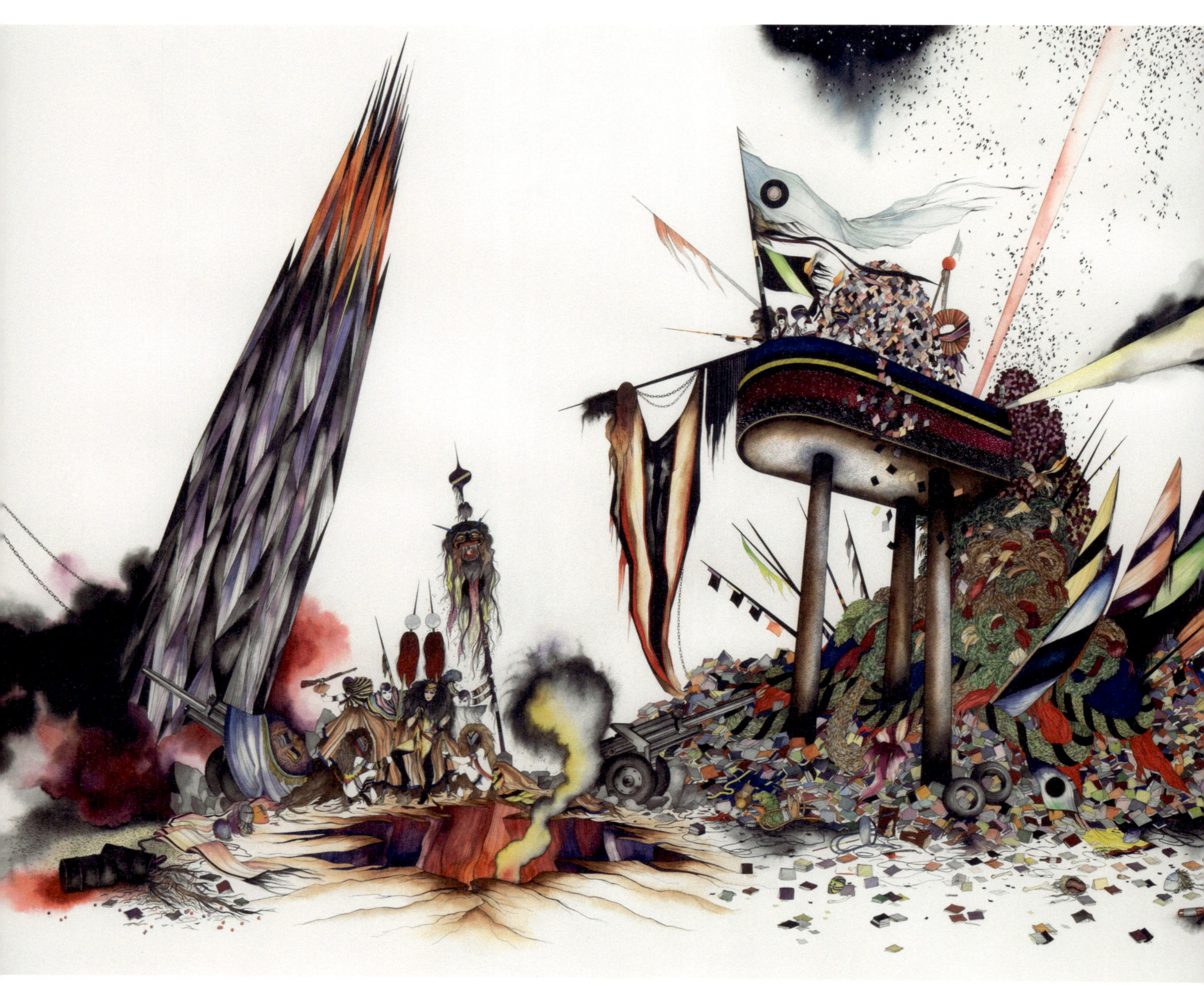

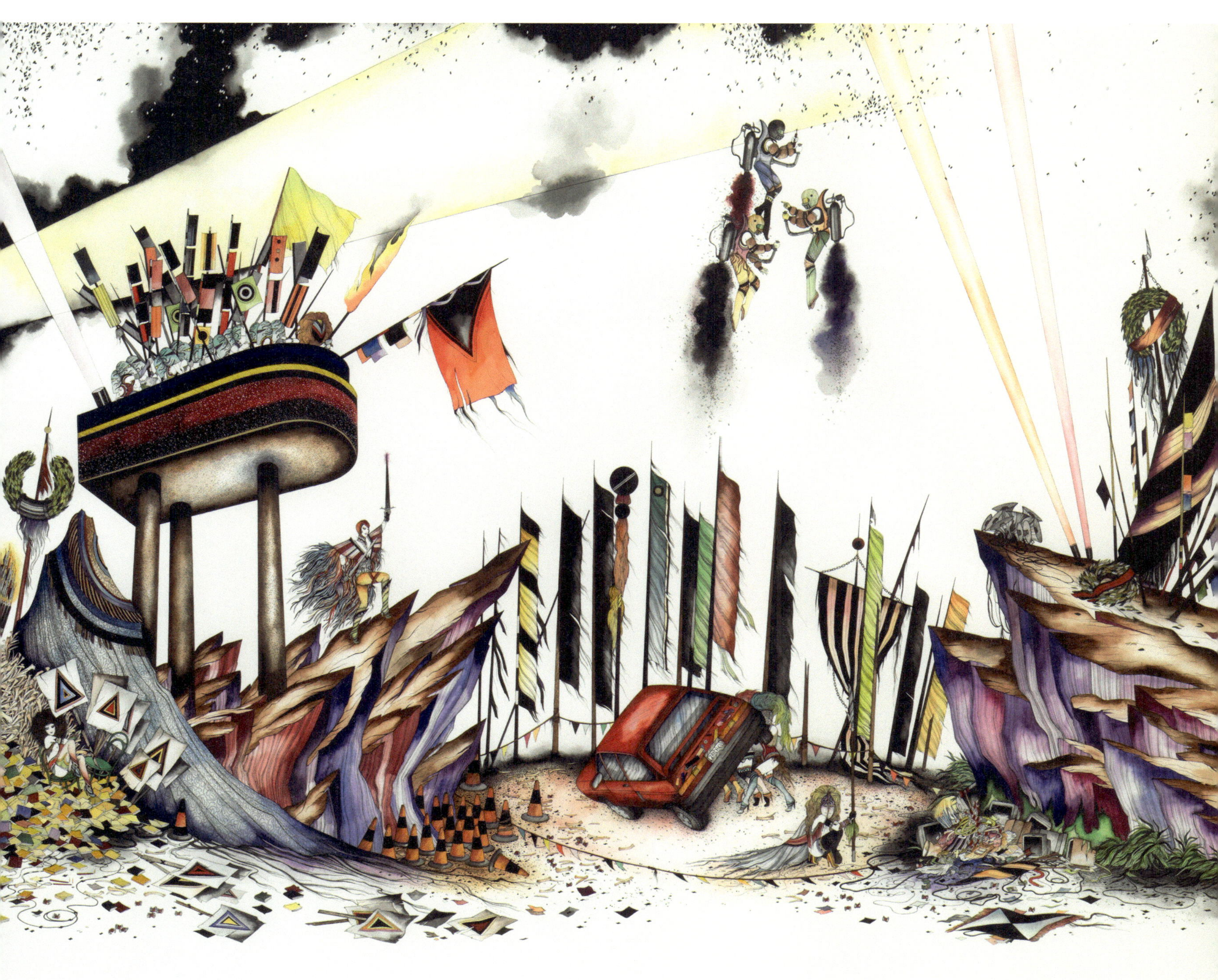

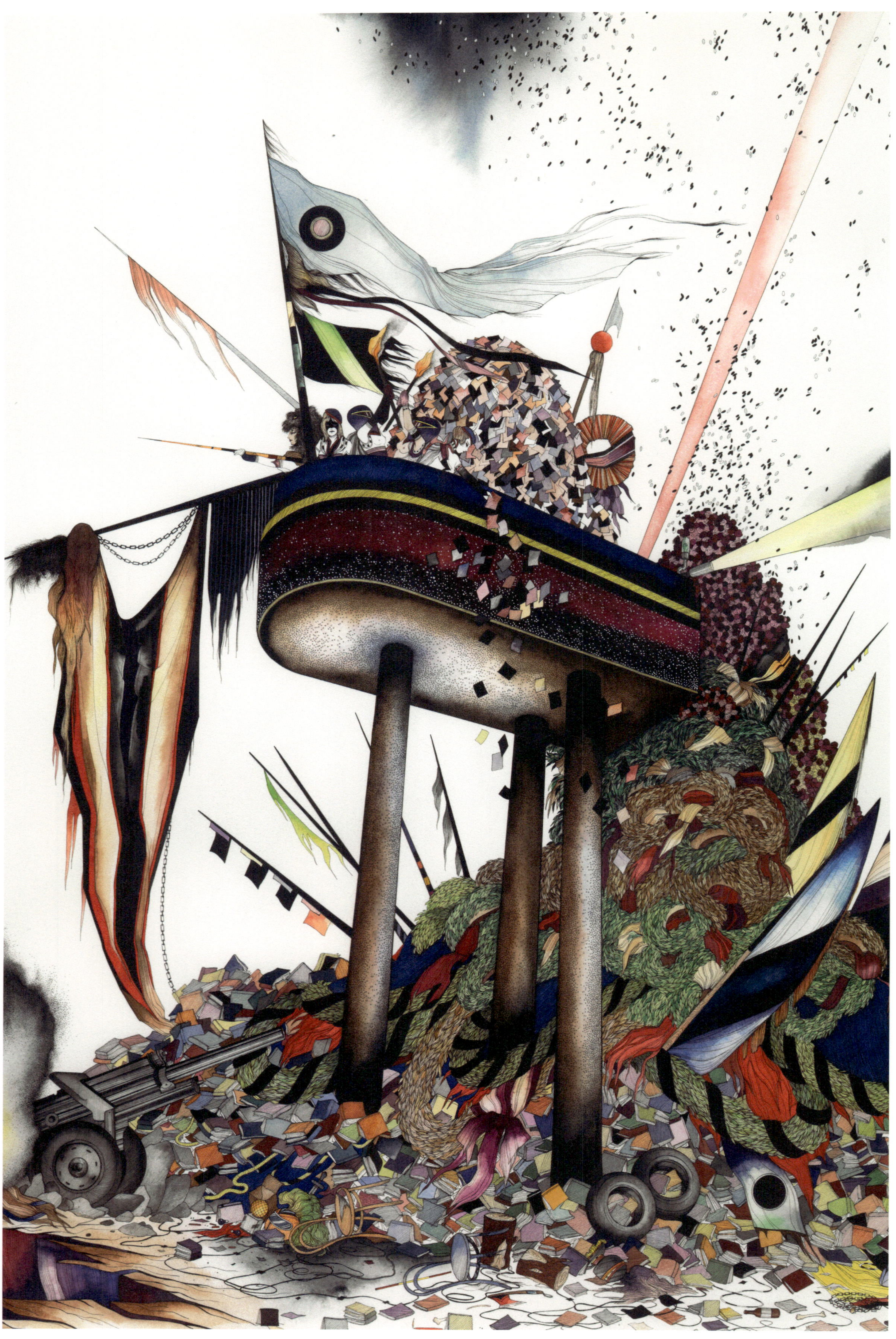

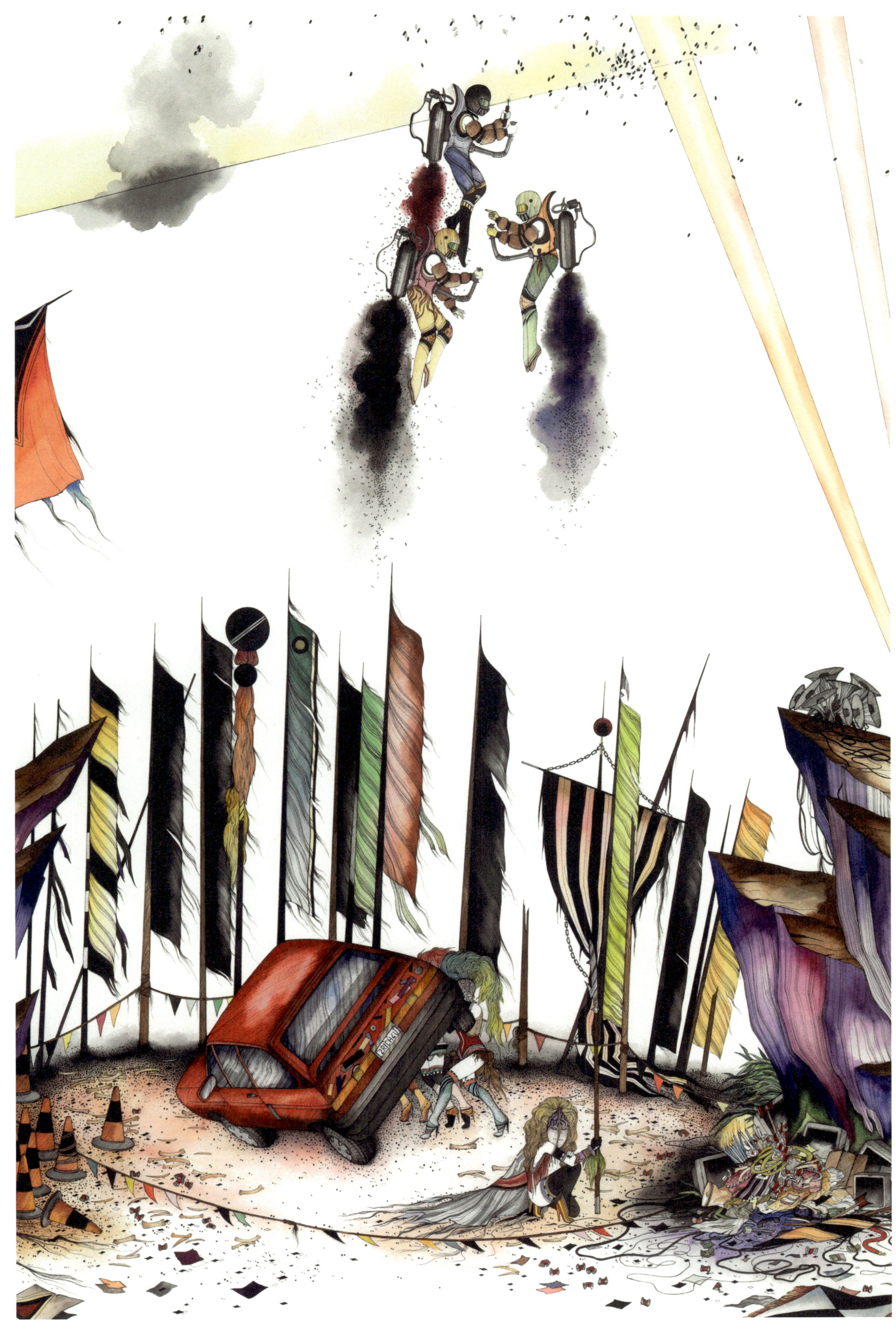

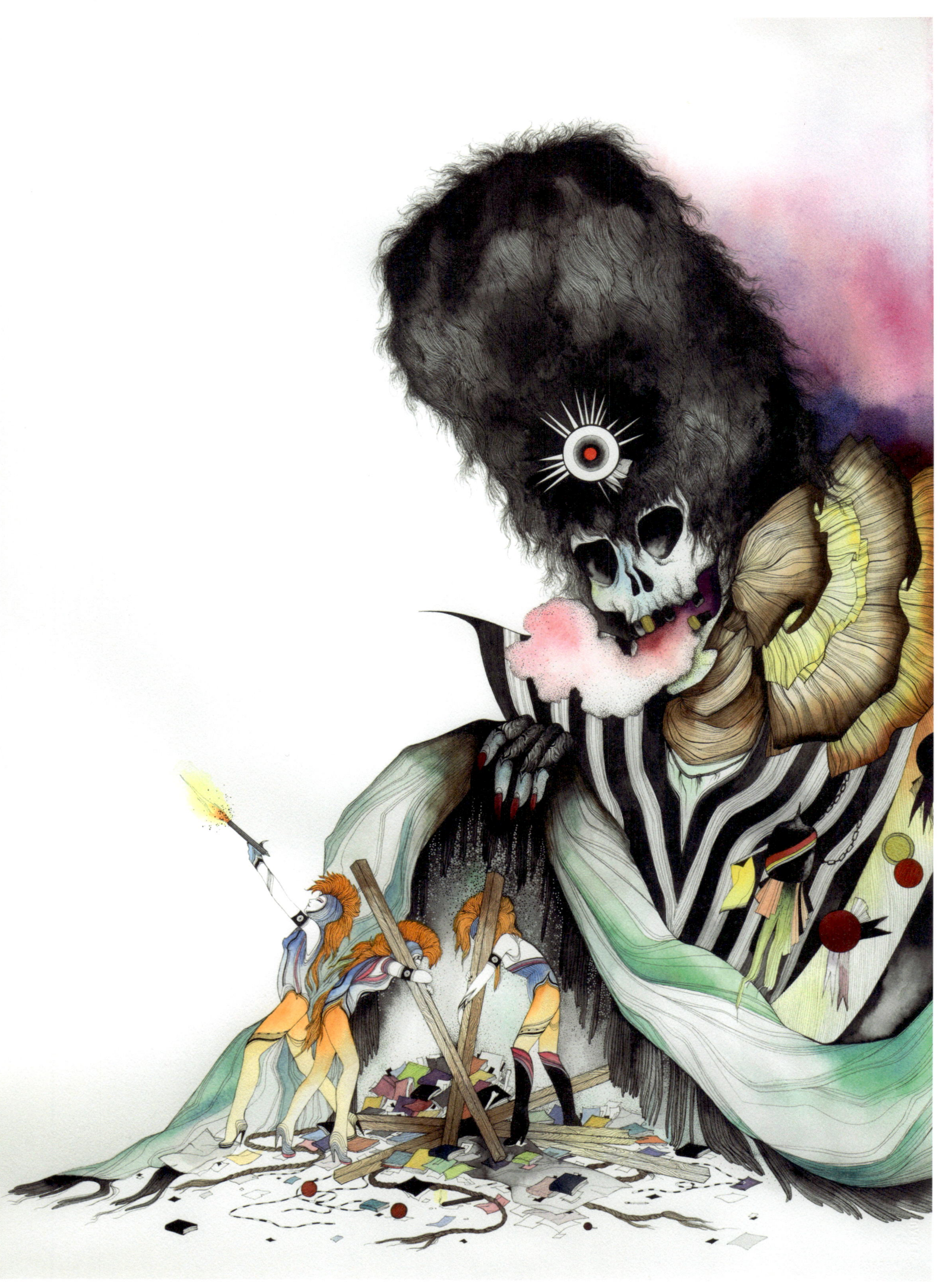

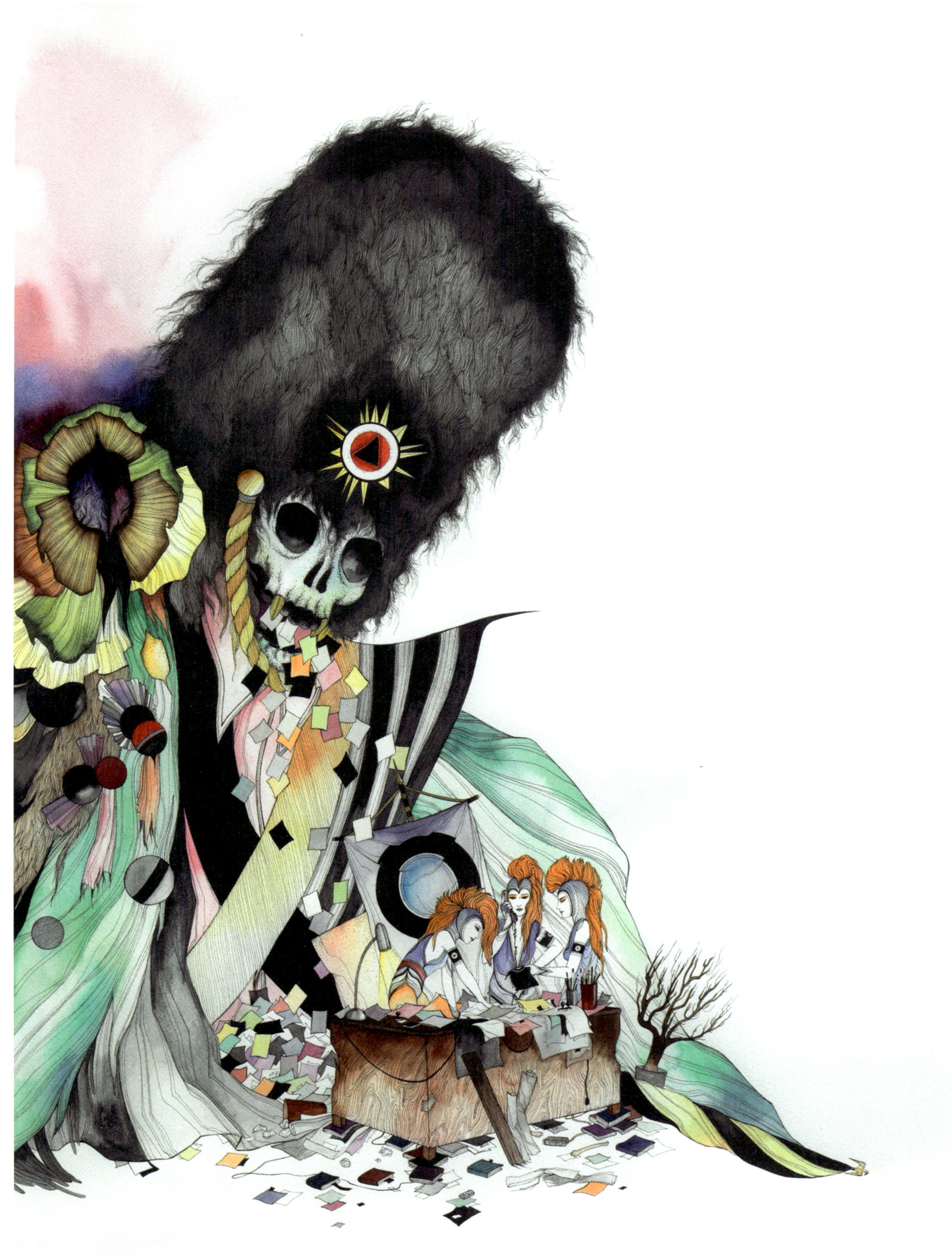

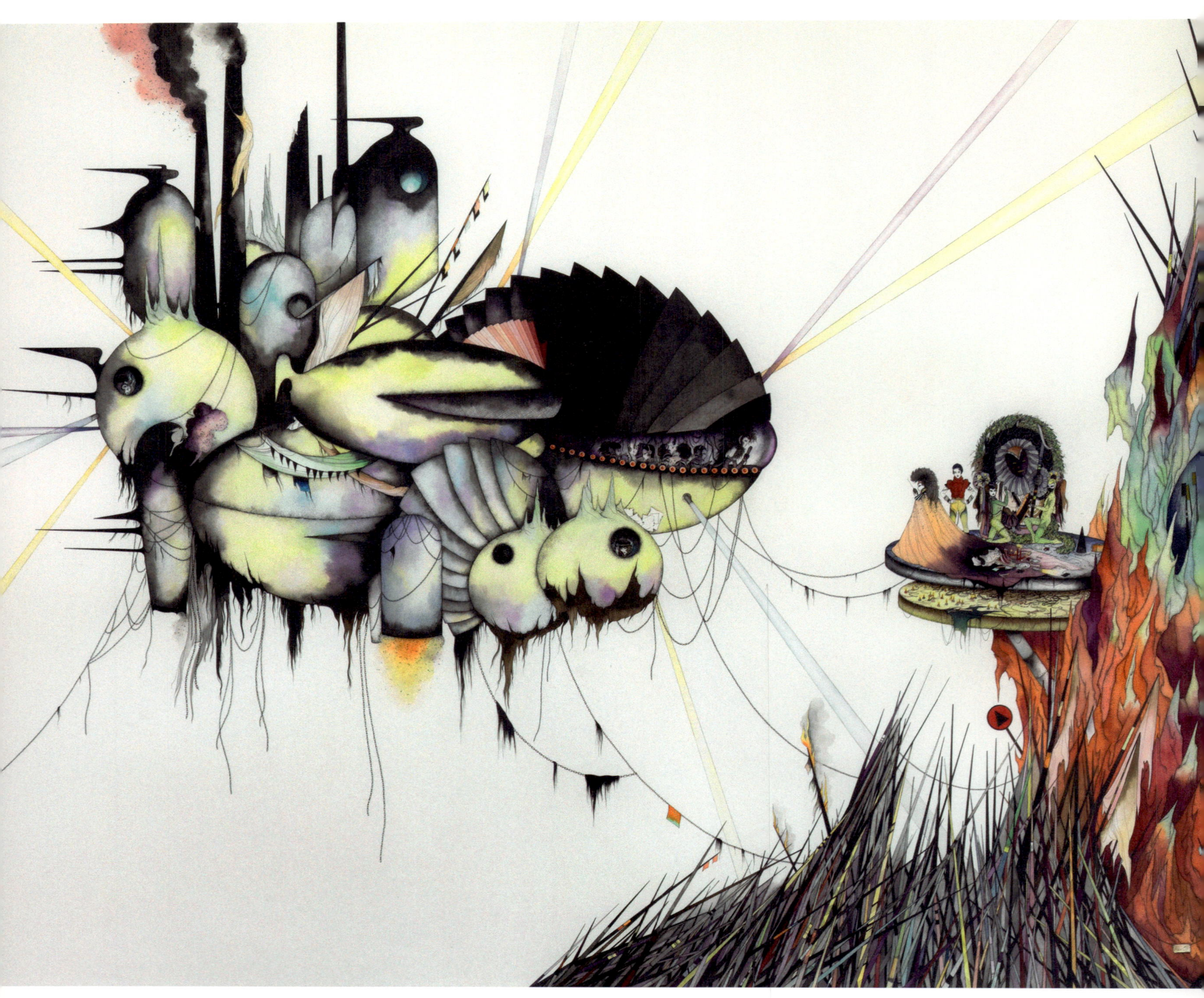

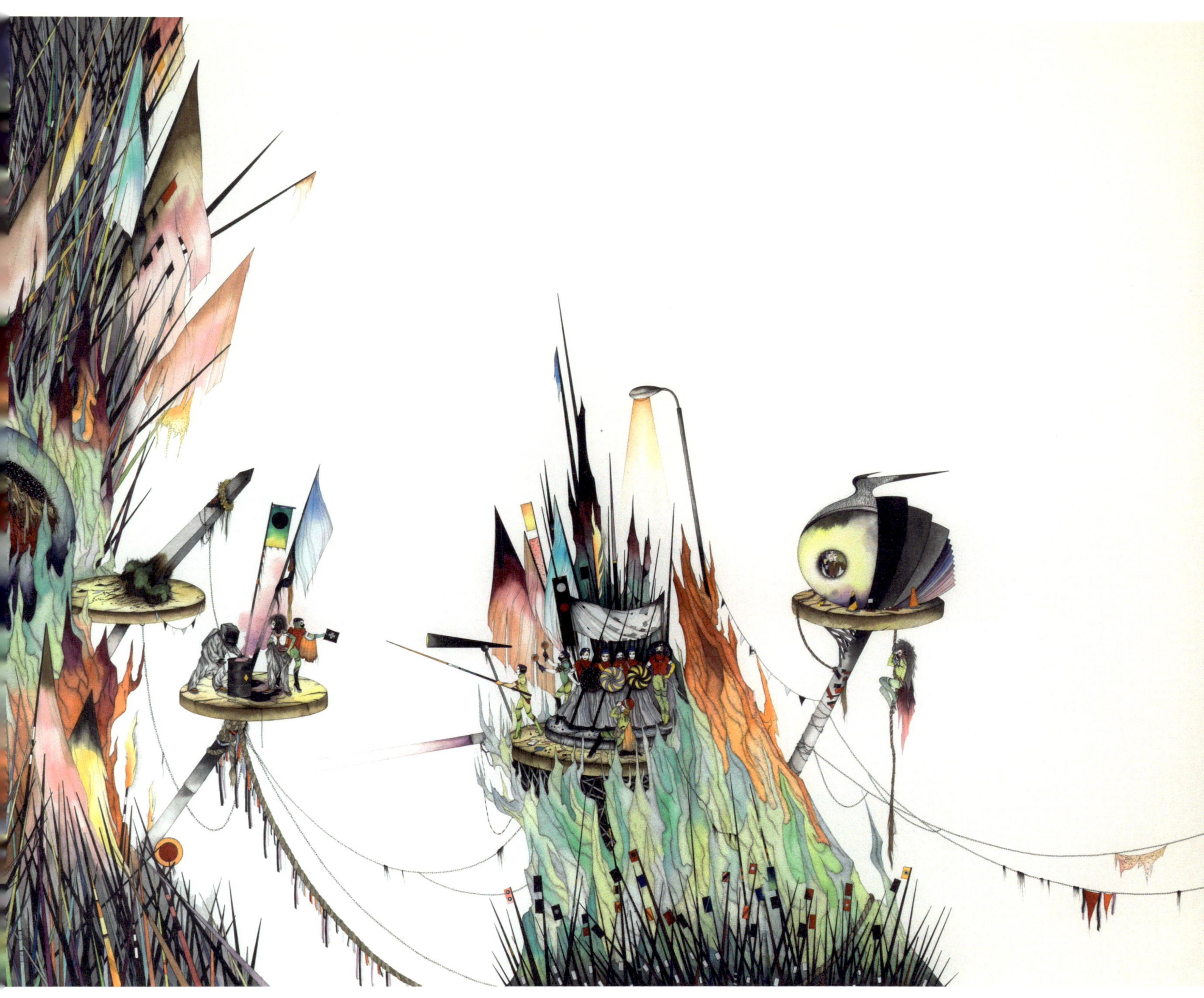

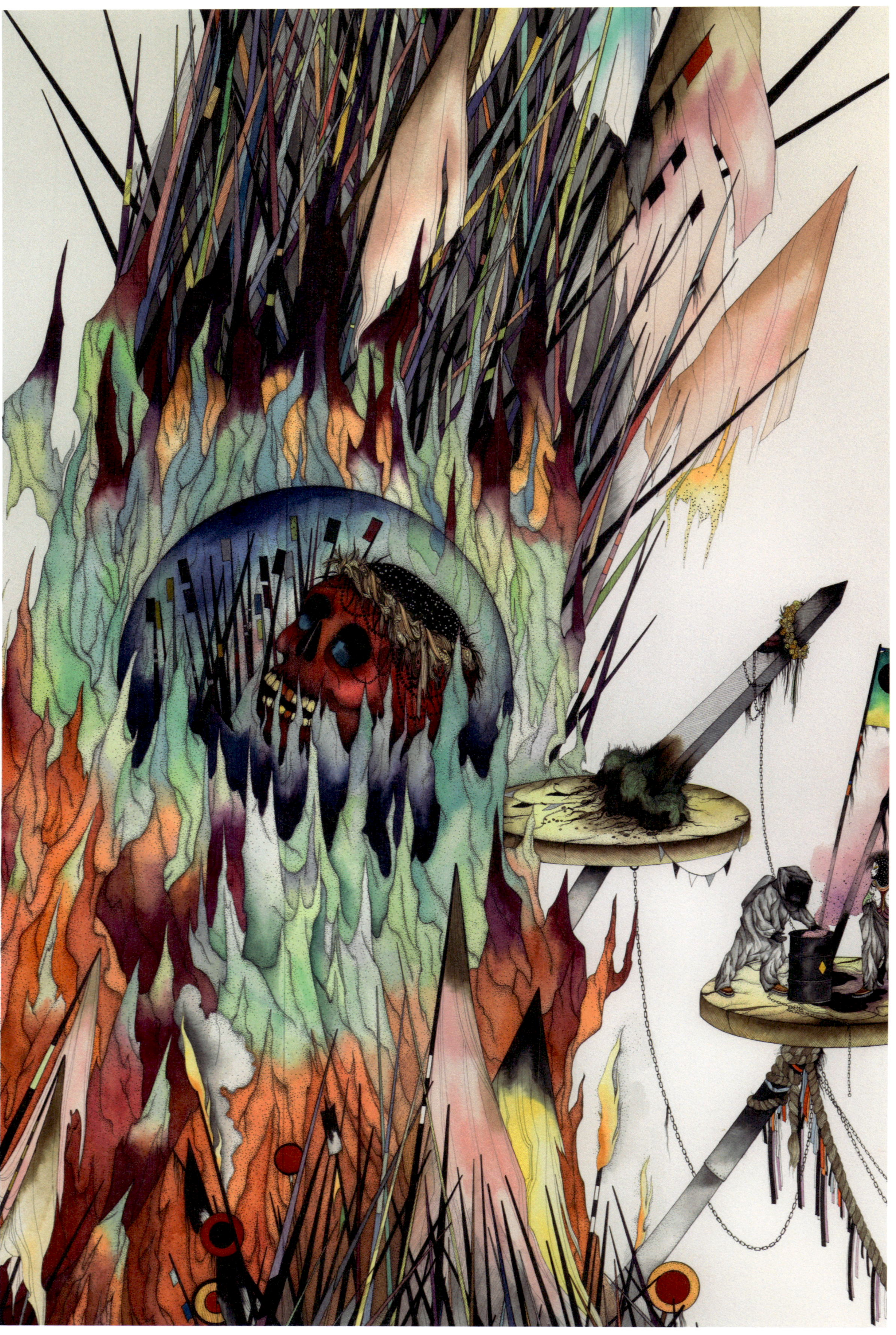

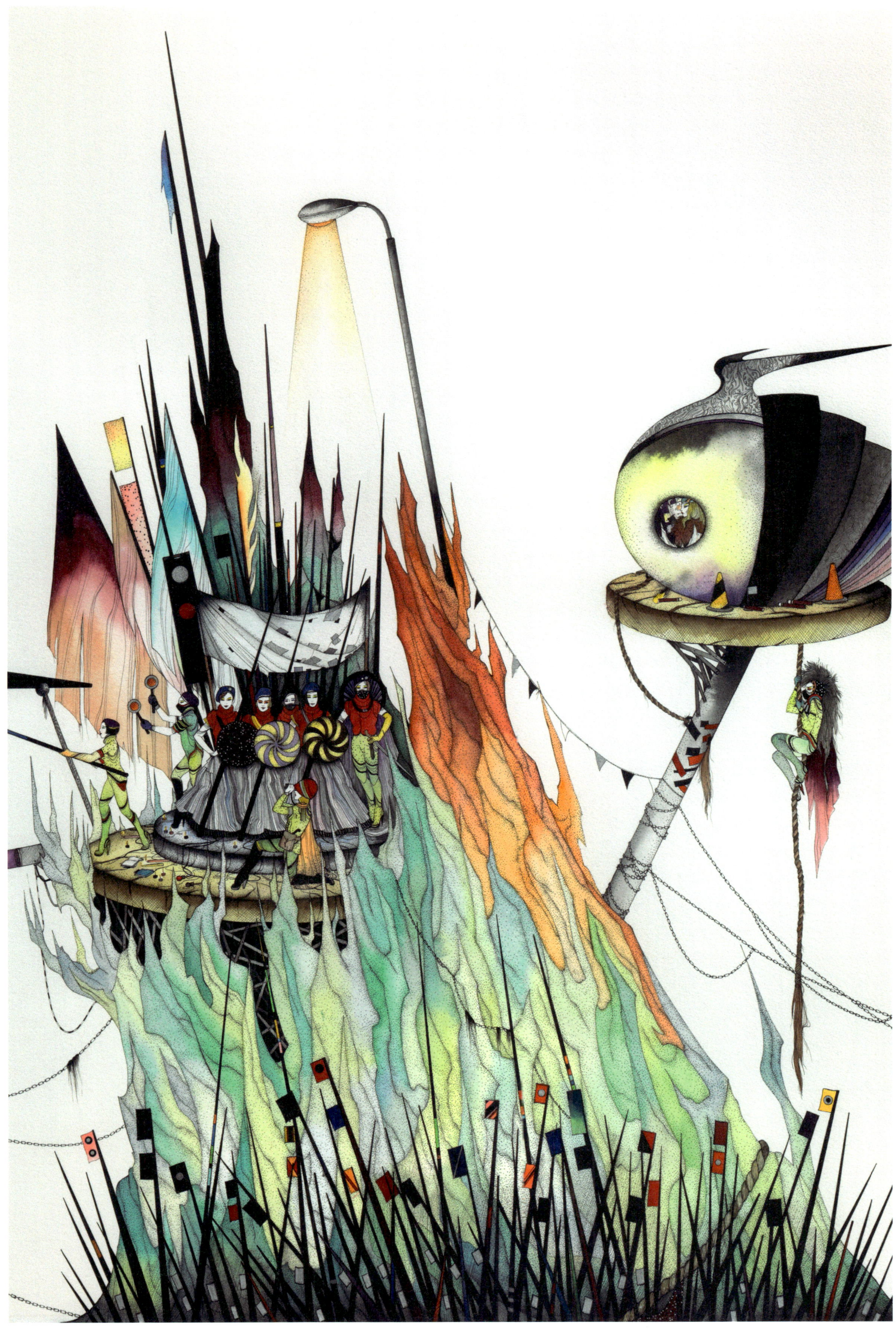

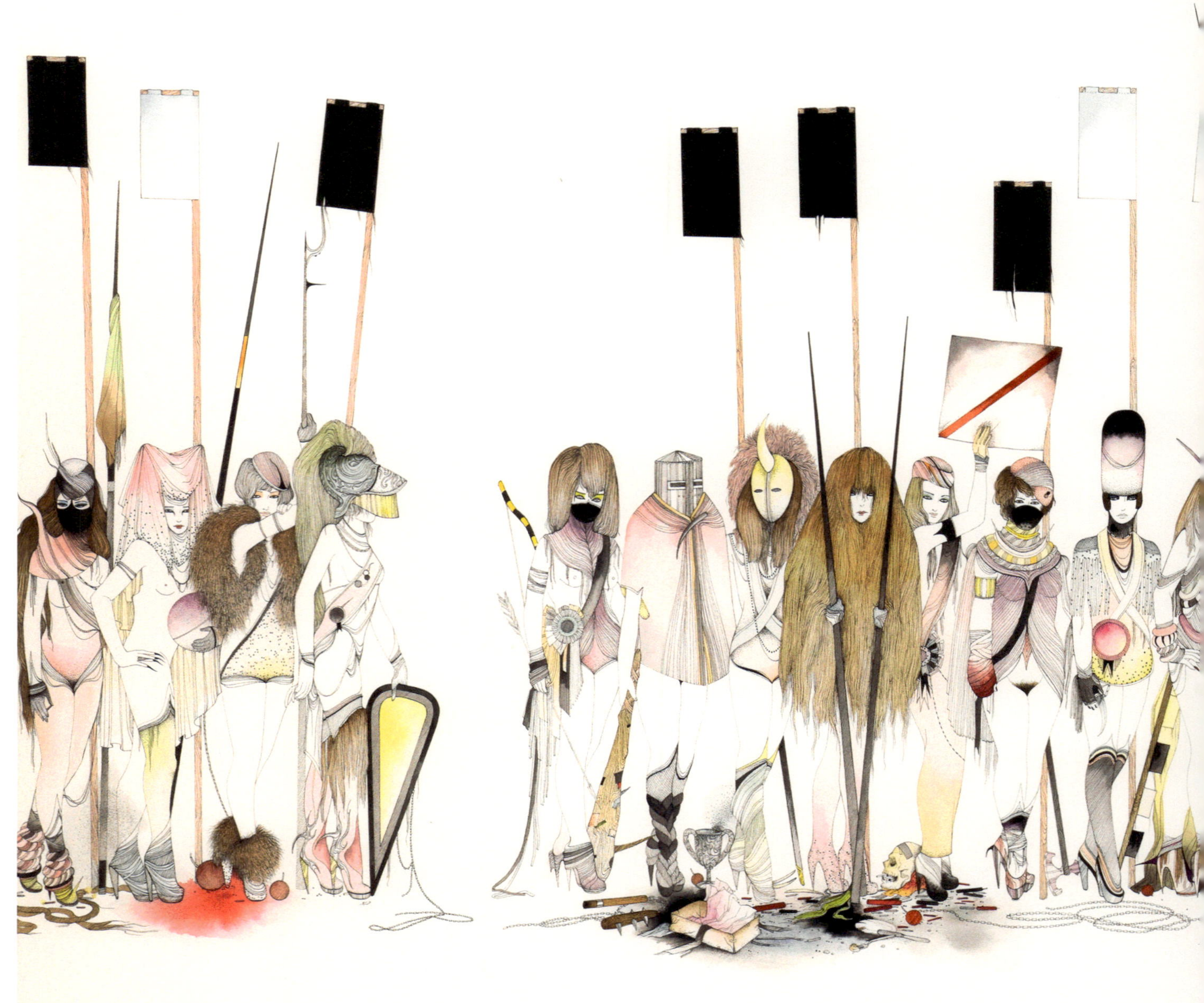

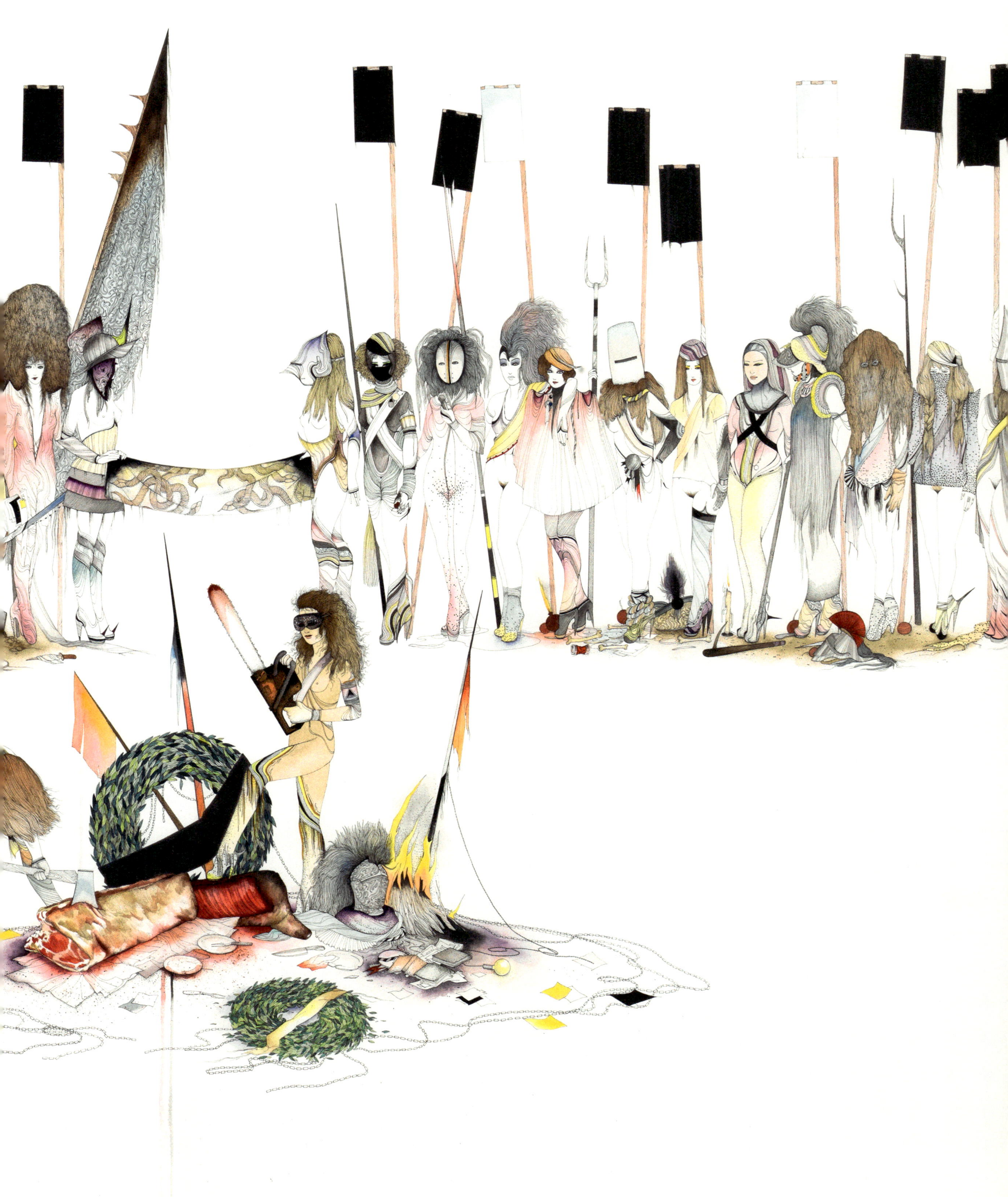

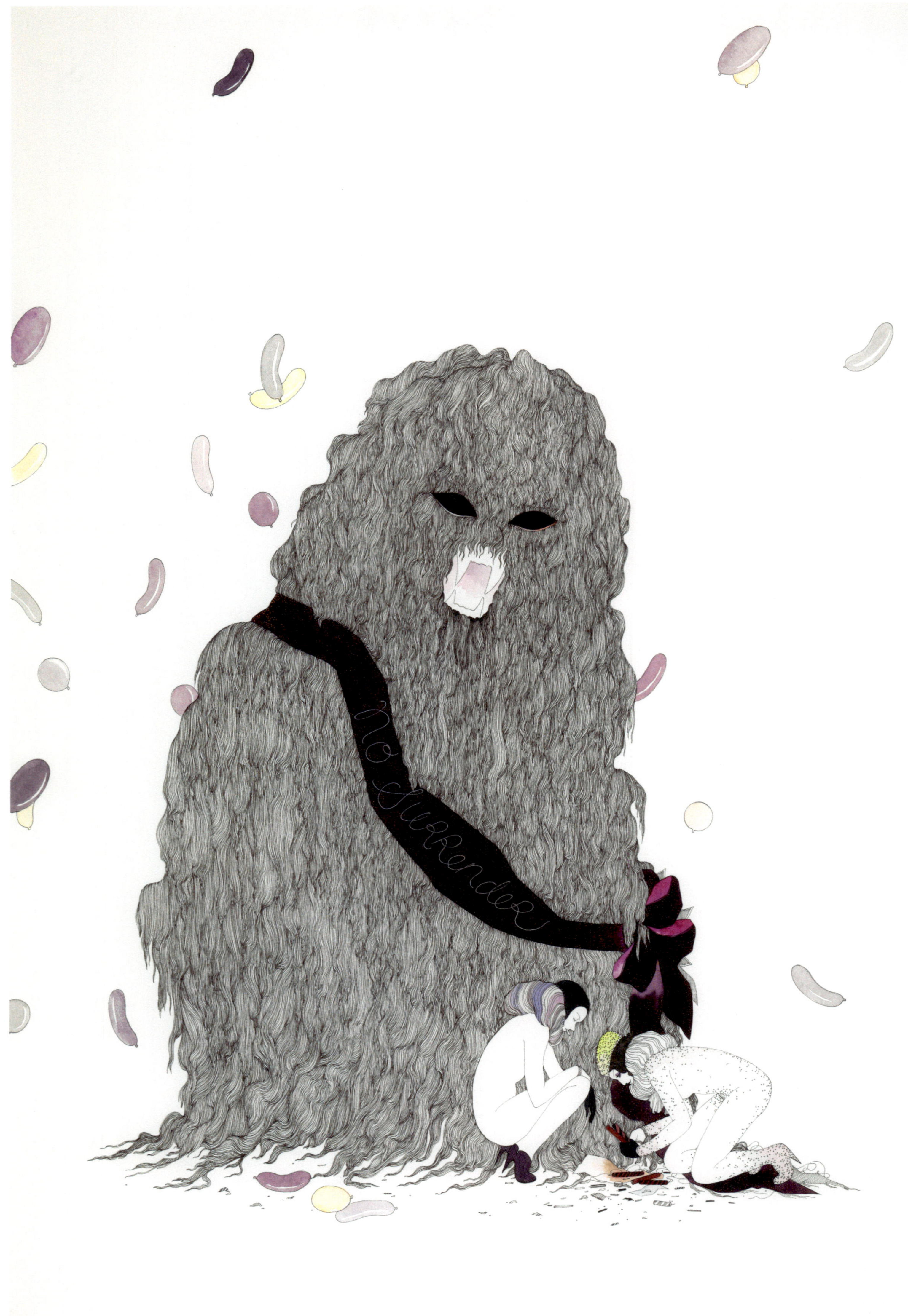
No Surrender

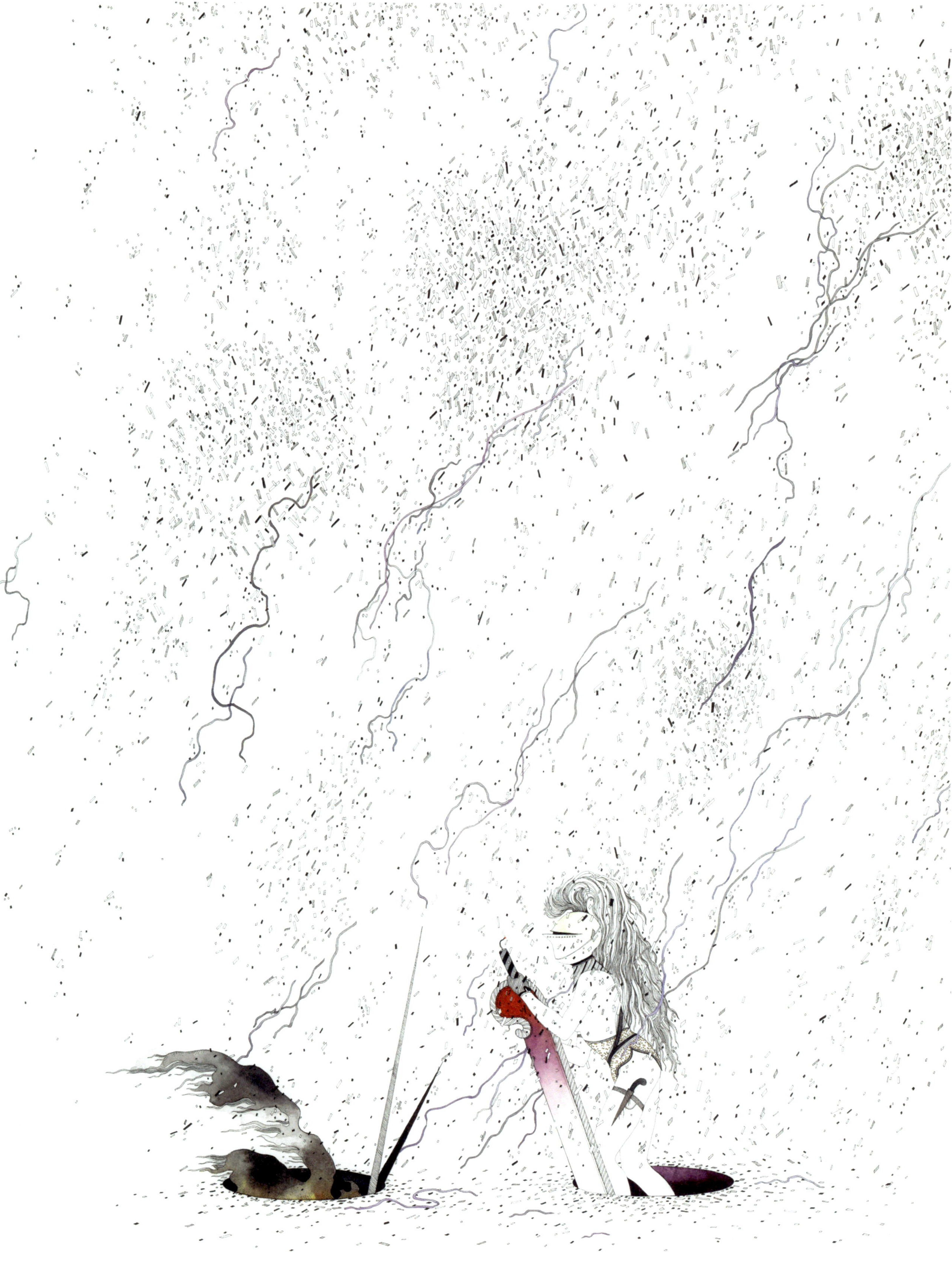

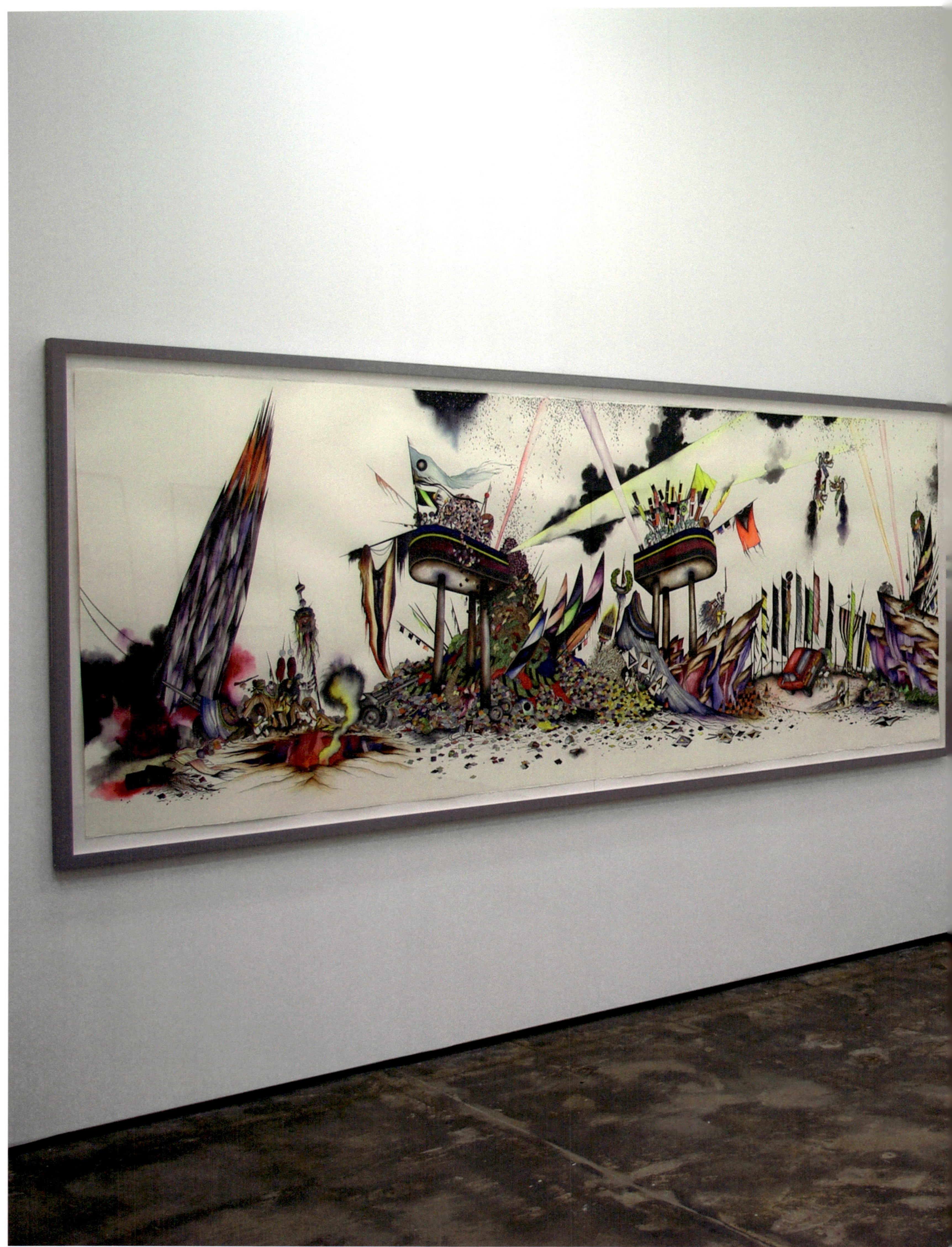

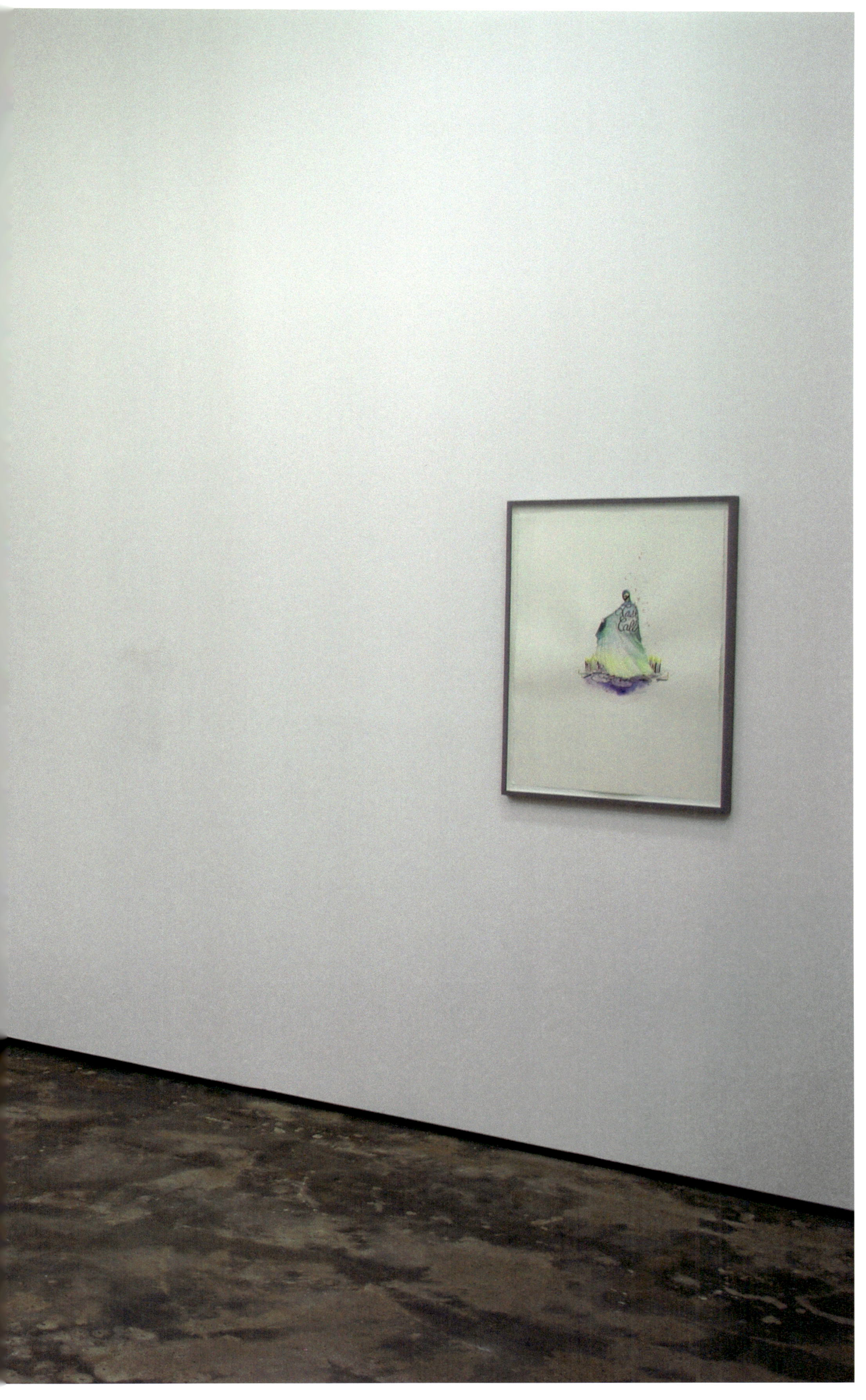

How would you articulate the tensions between opulence, decadence, and control in your work?

If you look at the pure definition of decadence, it refers to deterioration and decay, but when people refer to decadence, they are usually referencing over-the-top behavior. I deal with that in my work but I'm also interested in the breaking-down, be it positive or negative. The women populating my drawings are destructive, yet they create this world for themselves. They are the wild things, which can create negativity. Radicalism often means you risk decay. When you push boundaries they sometimes push back.

Anarchists rarely plan past their revolution.

Sure, they are more focused on the action. But my drawings always show the ramifications. There will be a beautiful structure depicted in my drawings with color and decoration, but somewhere you'll see the structure is crumbling. The destruction is part of my work. But I still want my characters to go forth and do what they need to do. I don't want to hold them back. I just want there to be that constant push-pull. I want viewers to see the same dichotomy in the small details hidden amidst the opulence. I want a dirty newspaper to be seen against a golden robe.

Tell me about how your performances relate to the paintings and drawings.

It was important to me when I began the performances to create something visual that directly related to the drawings. I wanted the viewer to get the impression of a drawing come to life. For my first performance, "Last Call," I gathered together a unique looking team of women and asked them to wear costumes that in some cases were militaristic and others more anachronistic looking, each slightly different. I surrounded them with color, smoke, candles, and glass. The main stage consisted of a full-sized utility vehicle. Ihu Anyanwu, a singer, performed Black Sabbath's "Sweet Leaf." One of my main concepts was that I wanted a woman to sing a love song to an object instead of to a man. The performer sang it with intensity but she sang it to herself and to the women around her. No pandering to the audience! Each woman was directed to look straight ahead as if she couldn't have cared less about the audience.

Do you feel that most love songs objectify the "object" of the singers' affections?

A lot of them do and also they objectify "love" as a very specific concept.

It's strange how people project so much of themselves onto the object of their affection and are moaning away about "Cecilia" or "My Sharona" who are supposedly based on real people. I'm sure if you met the real-life person you would think they were nice enough but wonder if they really rated all that excitement? Maybe even they would say no.

What do you mean by "unique looking"?

I wanted all types of women included in the performance. Blonde, brunette, thin, tall, different ethnicities, etc. I know a wide range of women so this was easy.

The women in your drawings are pretty standard babes. How does their beauty relate to the qualities that compel you to work with a woman in the performances?

In the drawings and performances I consider beauty as a type of costume or even as armor so this is particularly important to me. All the women in the performance are attractive in real life but in the performance this is heightened by theatrical elements such as lighting, make-up, and costuming. I think I have a good eye for who can be transformed. It's also important that the women be interesting in real life too. I don't use models because they seem too empty to me. I like using people I know personally because I know their interests and thoughts and ideas.

And I definitely don't think that you have to be young and skinny to be considered attractive. Actually, I have a new project and I hope that my main performer will be in her late 70s!

What do the audiences signify for you? Are they interactive or are they just spectators?

I never consider the audience when I am planning something, be it a performance or an exhibition. It just never occurs to me. I'm always a little surprised by the crowds at a performance to be honest. I do tell the performers to treat the crowd as if they are mere observers. Also, if someone gets in your way, give them a bit of a shove and no ingratiating smiling or an "excuse me." Is it my fault if someone can't get out of the way of a woman with a spear?

I have had some funny reactions from the audience afterwards though. Someone once asked me where I found the performers for my performance "Barbelo." They were under the impression that the women were related somehow or also that maybe they were transsexuals.

What about the opulence? What does it signify besides a counterpoint to decay?

The opulence goes along with the decadence of course. That follows a certain artistic tradition. However, part of the pleasure of drawing for me seems to be depicting these rich layers upon layers upon layers. Or drawing some minute detail. It's a compulsion. At the same time, all of the items, no matter how small, have a particular meaning for me.

Isn't the real counterpoint to the decadence and decay not the opulence but your characters' regimented rituals? Both opulence and decay evoke chaos, whereas your characters are paragons of control. What frightens them?

Not much. I think they are too worldly. I find that people are more fearful and nervous in smaller places where change comes slowly. Sometimes you go to a small town and people are freaked-out, but in big cities people are more relaxed because they think they've seen it all or maybe they're just a bit more cynical about the world.

R
CA
OF
ME
YOU
DE

DI~
SM
EN
NS
RISK
AY

Your women hardly seem interested in their individual or selfish desires.

Yes and no. I'm interested in regimented action but you'll notice that I almost always break that up. If I show an army of women then their uniforms will never be entirely the same. I'll set them apart. One figure may have even decided not to join in the group and can be seen reading a newspaper or having a glass of wine. In a real army that's grounds for a court marshal, in mine it's a character who has decided for the moment to go her own way. I'm interested in the rhythmic effect of formation and the sense that the women are trying to accomplish something as a group, but I am compelled to break it up. I don't necessarily think of militaristic behavior as always being a negative but there are enough negatives associated with it, such as blind conformity, that I must always counter it somehow.

Artists perhaps think of these behaviors as inherently negative because their general lifestyles and temperaments are less structured – not less disciplined but less structured.

Maybe, but like many military people I do believe that human life involves degrees of fighting and conflict. However, it also involves some waiting around for the action to occur. Within the drawings, there are people reading the news or listening to the radio because the women should be informed before taking action. Maybe that is a somewhat liberal artistic attitude.

Something that also interests me as an artist is the radicalization of people beyond general conflict. Someone who has decided to step outside the social structure of their community. Something so extreme that it changes their relationship to the rest of humanity.

Are the women in your performances people whose work or personalities exemplify your own attitudes towards expression and action?

Very much so. We talk about some of the actions and movements and concepts beforehand. I tell them what I want to accomplish, but they aren't robots. Some are actors and dancers, so they know what it's like to work with someone who has certain ideas to get across. However, some of them are writers and musicians with their own creative work. But working with these particular women is always fun because they are intelligent and grasp the ideas very easily.

So, why paint warrior women?

It's a bit of an anomaly, unless you think of Amazons. We don't normally think of women engaged in conflict however often we see images of female soldiers.

That's the one example, isn't it?

Another example would be several noted female samurai. One in particular was named Tomoe Gozen. She was supposed to be both beautiful and ferocious. My work is influenced by Japanese scroll paintings as well as Japanese history.

That's really evident in your imagery.

I discovered that there was something in Japanese society called onnaa-bugeisha which were Japanese women of the upper classes who were samurai. While the warrior husband was away, someone had to defend the land and the castle and the servants and the children.

But it was more of a novelty than a society. Like the WACS or WAVES. There are lots of individual female radicals in history but rarely a unified female army.

True, but there are often female groupings that I consider. Take the example of the parade queen and her court riding on a float. The queen is the beautiful girl in the center. Traditionally she has on a white dress that symbolizes her purity. She wears a red sash and crown to signify the importance of her position. She has her court gathered around her and she is waving gently to the crowds. It is a very particular way of looking at womanhood. I am interested in taking a group of women like that and upending it. My queen is never wearing white and she may be holding a spear or a cudgel, her court may be throwing Molotov cocktails or radioing for backup.

The funny irony is that these women are usually pretty brutal bitches with each other. We've all seen enough satires and exposés to know that these little girly courts are far from sisterly. They are competitive and hyper-aggressive. But the goal that they're all fighting for is the chance to represent an utterly antithetical ideal.

Yes, that's true oftentimes. The women I'm depicting have solidarity and group purpose. I wouldn't want to think of them as anti-sisterly. Brutal bitches yes, at cross purposes, no.

There is a lot of physical aggression being realized in your works but interestingly, there doesn't seem to be a lot of psychological violence between the girls.

I have these rules for myself. I don't want to depict women negatively. I don't want to show a woman down on the ground or hurt. I don't want to show a woman being subservient. There are certain poses that I avoid – I'm into empowerment. It's a somewhat cheesy word but I'm showing these women as powerful people who know their own minds. They know what they want and they are out to get it, whatever that might be. I don't judge them.

It is really a shame that "empowerment" has become a corrupted or trivialized term. It's so easy for these genuinely powerful terms and references to become neutralized and disempowered by being misappropriated or just popularized.

Yes, and if you simply use the word "power" it's incorrect. I'm not into mere "power." It is more complex and multi-layered than that. Also, the women in my paintings are something like alter egos. I think a lot of artists are voyeurs and they create characters to represent something that they want to do in life. That to me is a type of empowerment as well.

Some of your visual reference points have gone through a similar process as words like "empowerment." When would you decide that metal or pin-up is too trendy to have real meaning?

As far as pin-ups, I think that my characters maintain something more original and tougher than your average pin-up. They are beautiful but they are not posing specifically for a viewer. This sets them apart.

And as for heavy metal, it's obviously seen as something very male, and the artists in the art world that are invested in it are mostly male. I sometimes depict elements of metal culture because like many people of a specific age I grew up with the original aesthetic. I always felt like an outsider though because girls were not supposed "get it," let alone play a guitar or wear the standard "metal uniform" of sleeveless tour t-shirt and ripped jeans. I wanted to feel closer to the metal aesthetic through my work but I can't say that it's turned out that way. Or rather I don't think that people particularly pick up on that.

What about the women who were part of it, like Lita Ford or even Joan Jett?

There are those anomalies rearing their heads again! I love those women and I do think I use pieces of them in the drawings and especially the performances. For one thing they had much better outfits than their male counterparts. I've been depicting women in costumes from way back. It's related to fashion as much as music. Since I was a kid, I drew one woman after another. One day my grandmother found my drawings and asked, "What is going on with you?" We had a huge blow-out. I honestly think that she thought I was a pre-lesbian. My cousin reminded me of it recently. She asked whether I remembered when Grandma flipped out over the drawings. And, of course, I remember it. I was completely traumatized! Although that didn't stop me obviously.

I'm surprised. All girls like women in costumes. That's why there is a doll industry. Who is Barbie, if not a woman in costume?

True. But there was something different about it that must have worried my grandmother. Lots of girls draw women in costumes, but it doesn't turn out to be an artistic profession. Something about it must have seemed strange to my grandmother.

What do you think your grandmother would think of your performances?

Ah, I'm not sure if I would even want her to see them. I don't think she would embrace it, that's for sure.

How are the costumes in the performances related to the clothes worn by the women in the drawings?

I create the costumes for the drawings from my imagination but with the help of costume books, movies, vintage magazines, and various other outside influences. Then, for the performances I visit prop and movie costume shops and assemble various items that resemble the costumes in my drawings. Recently I've partnered with different fashion designers here in Berlin. That's been interesting for me as well.

What about fashion design and the fashion aspect of your art?

I've always been interested in fashion history and fashion design. But I want to take something about fashion and make it less passive. Women are often just hangers for clothes. That doesn't interest me. I look at fashion a lot and I'm inspired by it. But I want clothes that mean something and stand as active symbols.

Who is a designer who you think achieves that?

Sad to say but lately it's been Alexander McQueen. The combination of the futuristic and baroque in his last collection was thrilling.

Coupled with the off-putting animal imagery.

He was someone who was expanding his aesthetic past, the rarefied world of fashion into something more interesting. Also, his muses were two very interesting and eccentric women, Daphne Guinness and Isabella Blow. They represented something unique, not just blank-faced models.

I think that designers are most interesting when they, like McQueen, are not naturally members of that rarefied milieu. And, I am not only referring to class. I think it's fascinating when someone is designing for a body that's utterly different from their own. For McQueen, I imagine there were constant tensions between resentment, desire, envy, intimacy, and massive insecurity. How do you feel, as an artist, having collectors who live with your work but live such a different lifestyle than you do?

Rarely do people care about an artist's social station or even how they actually live. At least that's been my experience. I don't really think about the lifestyles of collectors. A lot of artists have very simple backgrounds, but find themselves in pretty high places. As far as my background, my family is middle class like a great many artists. I learned about art from my mother who is an artist but I never saw any "real art" until far past my childhood. I had never seen anything but a photograph of a painting in a book about art.

What did you see?

Ingres. It was a woman with big rubbery arms and a beautifully painted black dress. I think it was *Portrait of Madame Moitessier Standing.*

That makes perfect sense for you to see that. Ingres's fashion aspect is so strong. It's such a natural rapport with your work. What about Erté?

Ingres's work definitely relates to your observation about opulence in my work. Erté's women are beautiful but too decorative. It's my criticism about fashion in general. The women of Erté and Ingres seem trapped by their clothes and setting. Ingres in particular because the paintings are so leaden.

Returning to the topic of status and seeing my first piece of real art though, after seeing some really good pieces, the art itself became the important thing. The structure of the art world just seems more like something to adjust to. Maybe it's because of this that I've never been too concerned with art-world status and hierarchy.

Were you often blocked by status?

Not often, if at all. If you get caught up in that it will drive you crazy.

It's easier to push through social norms when you don't know what they are.

Also I subscribe to the American myth that anyone can catapult themselves to where they want to be, no matter what their background. It's practically a religion!

Your work really suits Berlin too. The issues of power, sexuality, and decay really do reflect a very Berlin aesthetic. Except that your medium isn't particularly Berlin.

I've always felt my medium to be very Berlin. I make watercolors featuring strong, sexual women imbued with street toughness that would just as soon cut you to look at you. At least that's how I think of them! Speaking of Berlin, the performance called "Barbelo," which was shown at the Akademie der Künste in 2009, was about female cabaret performers bridging the gap between theatricality and mysticism in Berlin, circa the late twenties, early thirties. Barbelo to me represents the emancipated woman of that time, drinking, dancing, and expressing herself "as a man would." Actually, I think a lot of women at the time were so over the top, for example Anita Berber, that to compare them to a man doesn't even begin to explain their behavior. And just so you know, Barbelo is also a Gnostic goddess with both male and female principles. The people who live here or know Berlin would say that this might be the perfect representation of the city.

Ana Finel Honigman is an art and fashion critic living in London and Berlin.

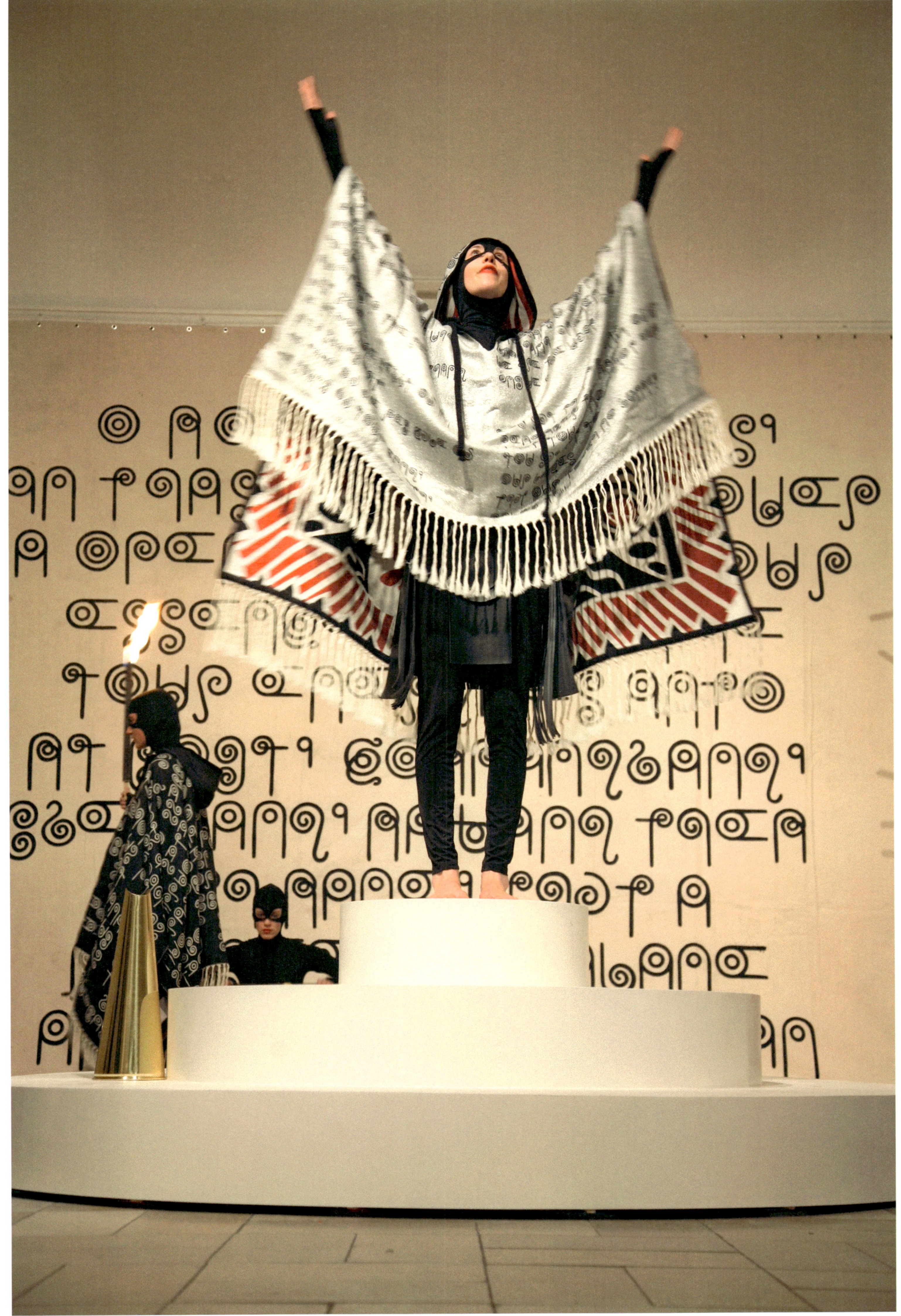

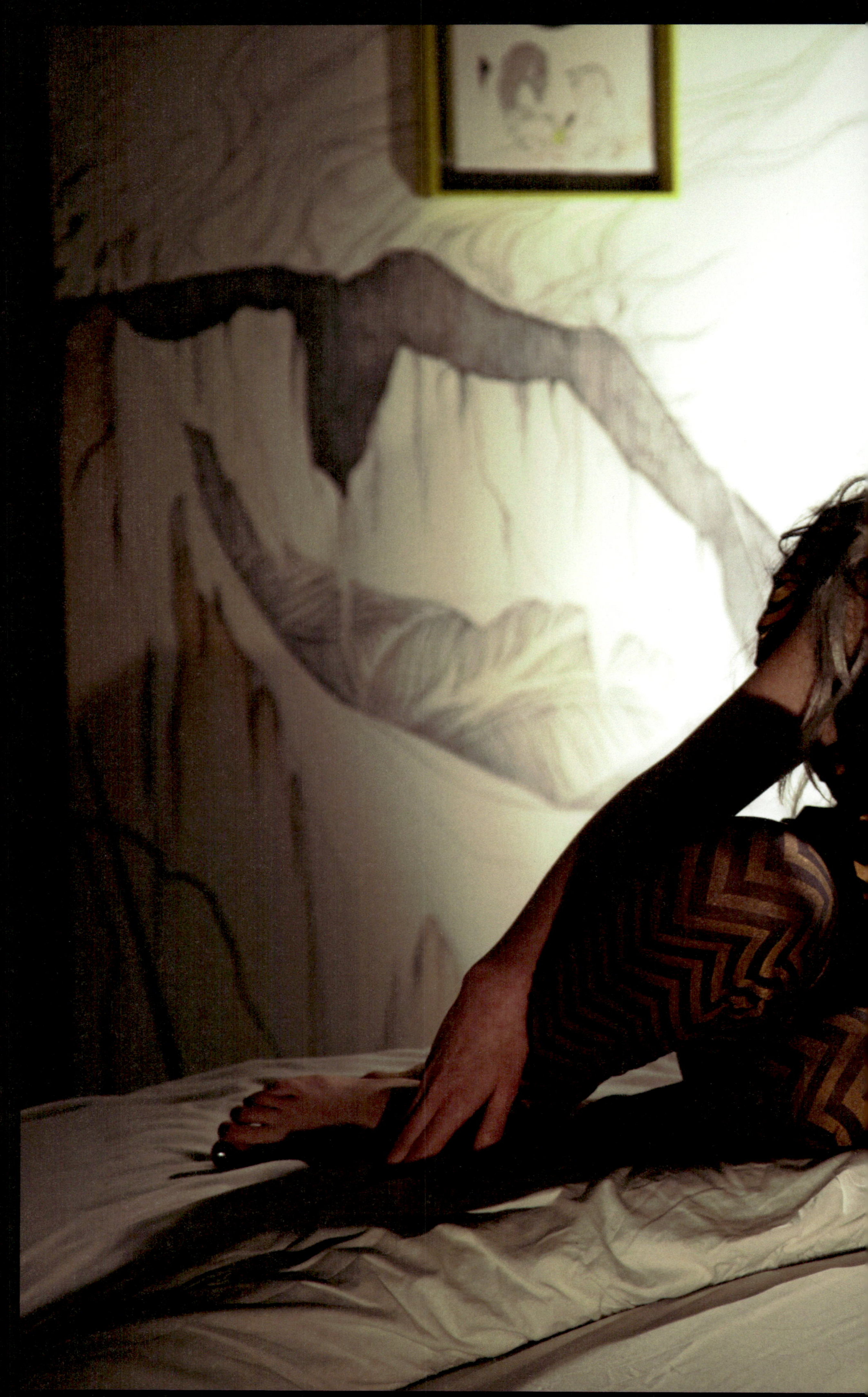

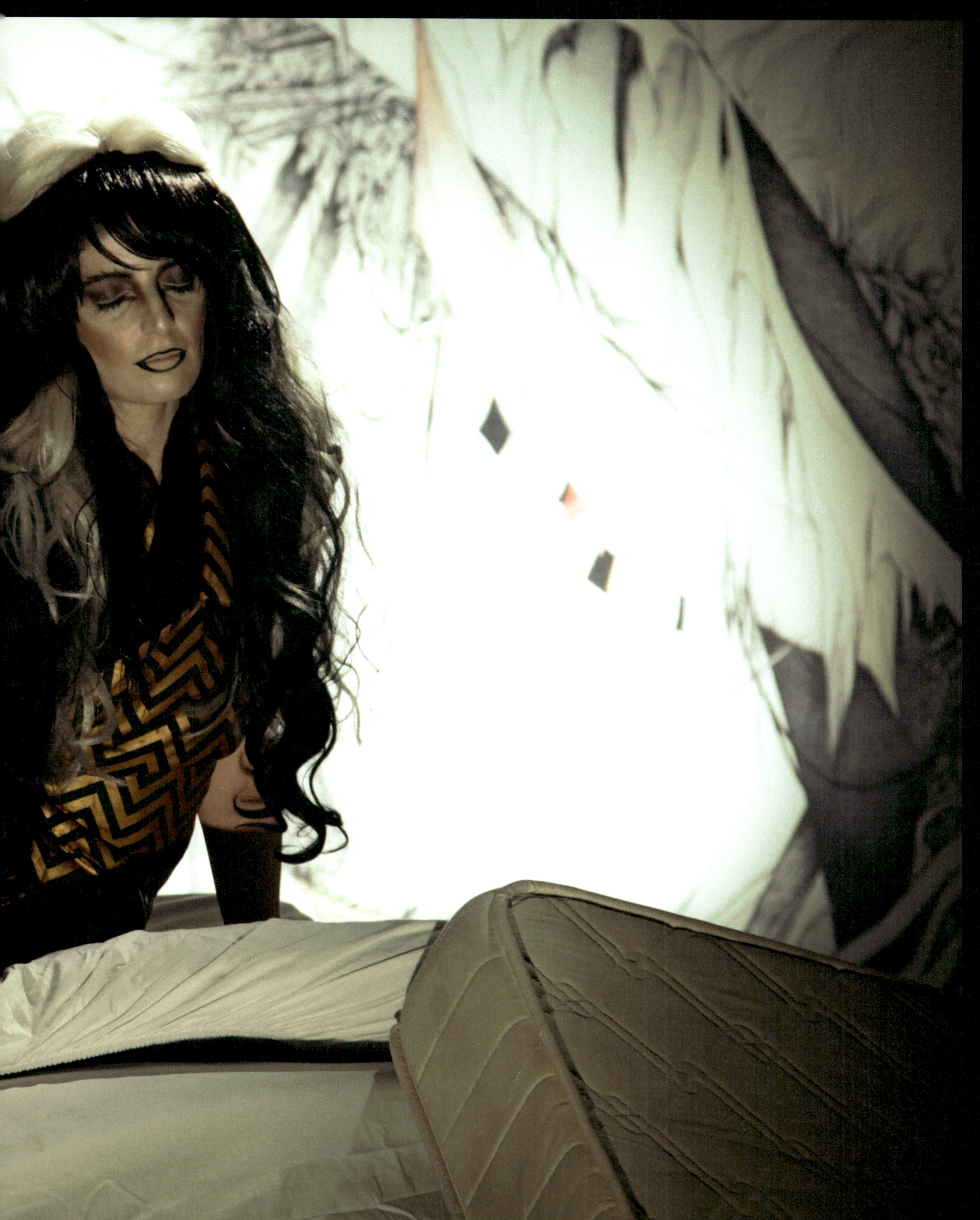

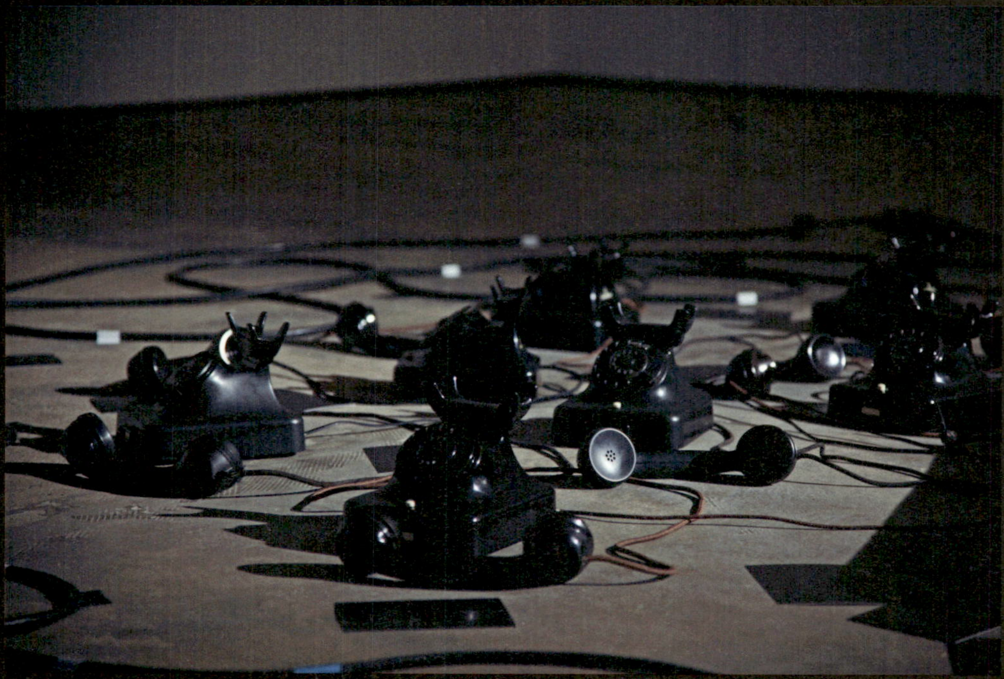

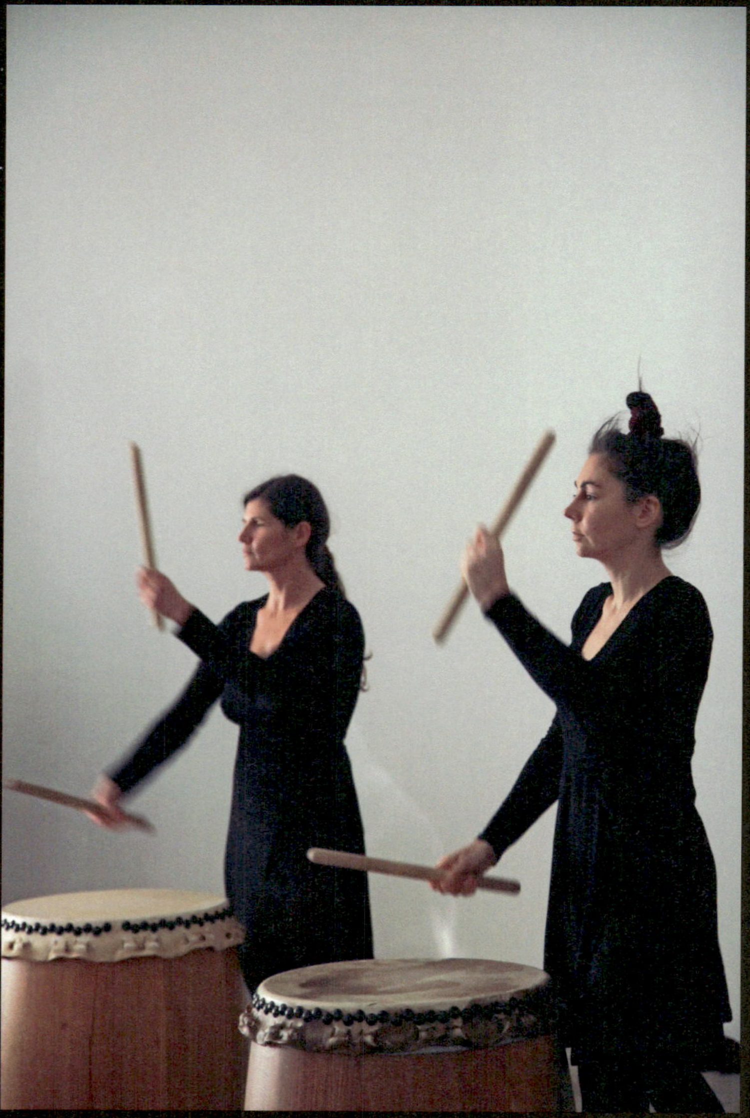

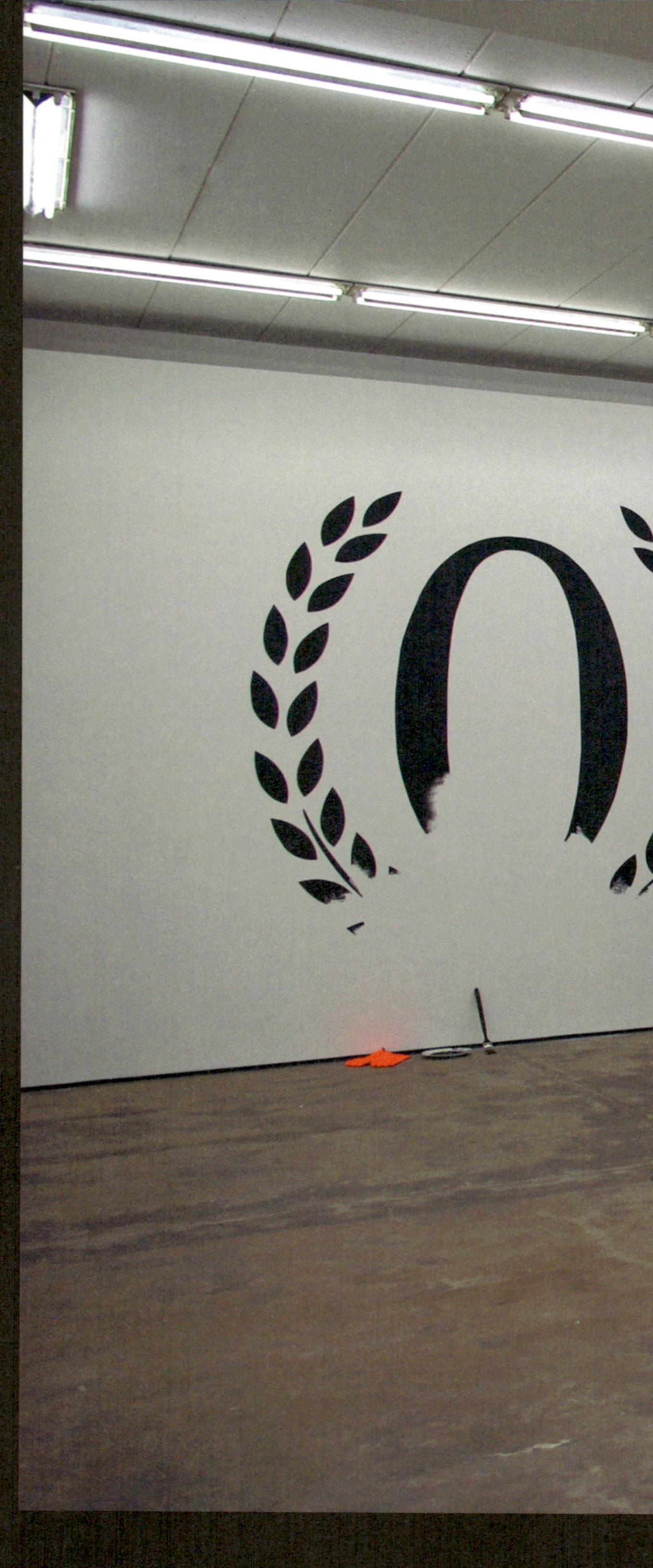

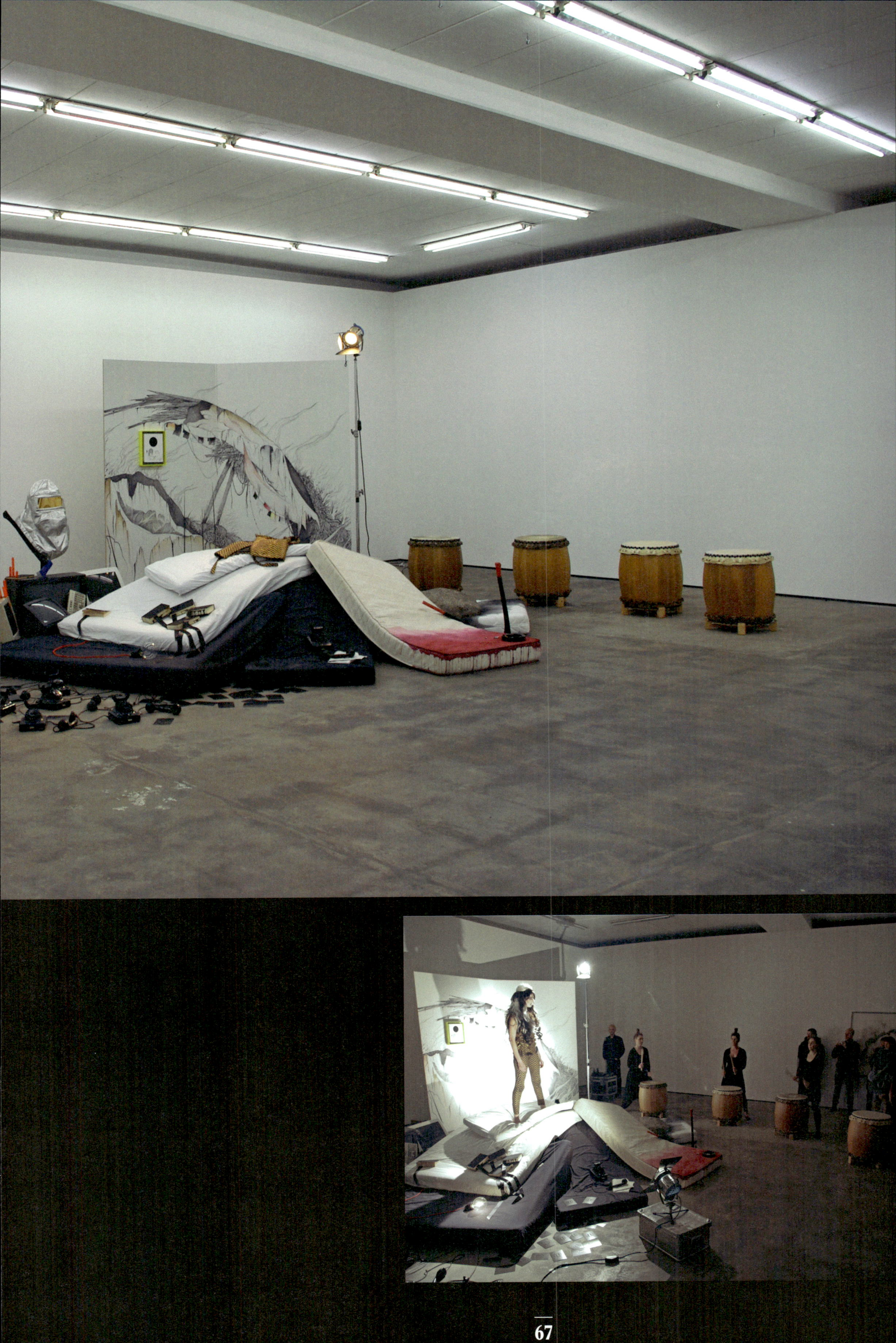

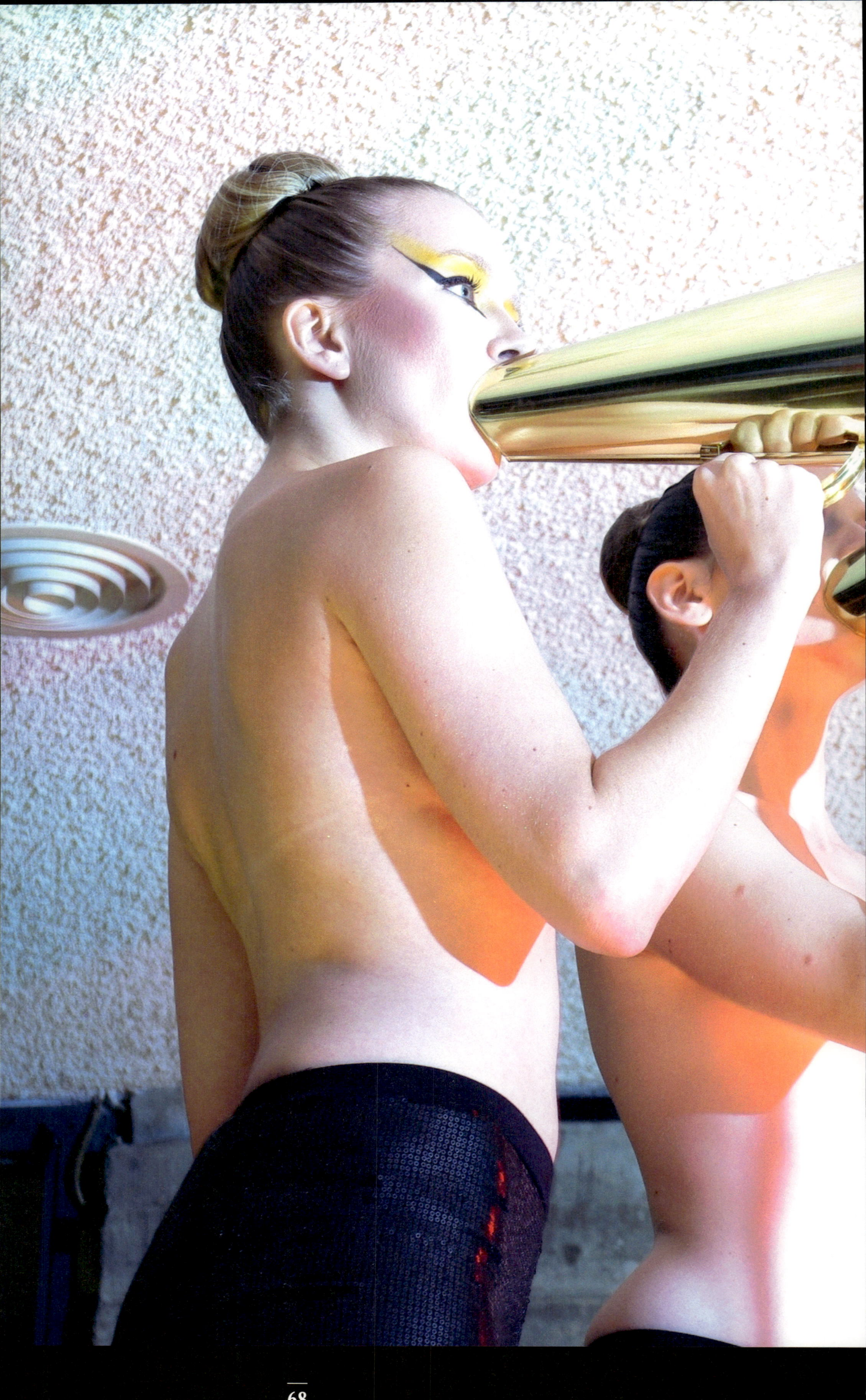

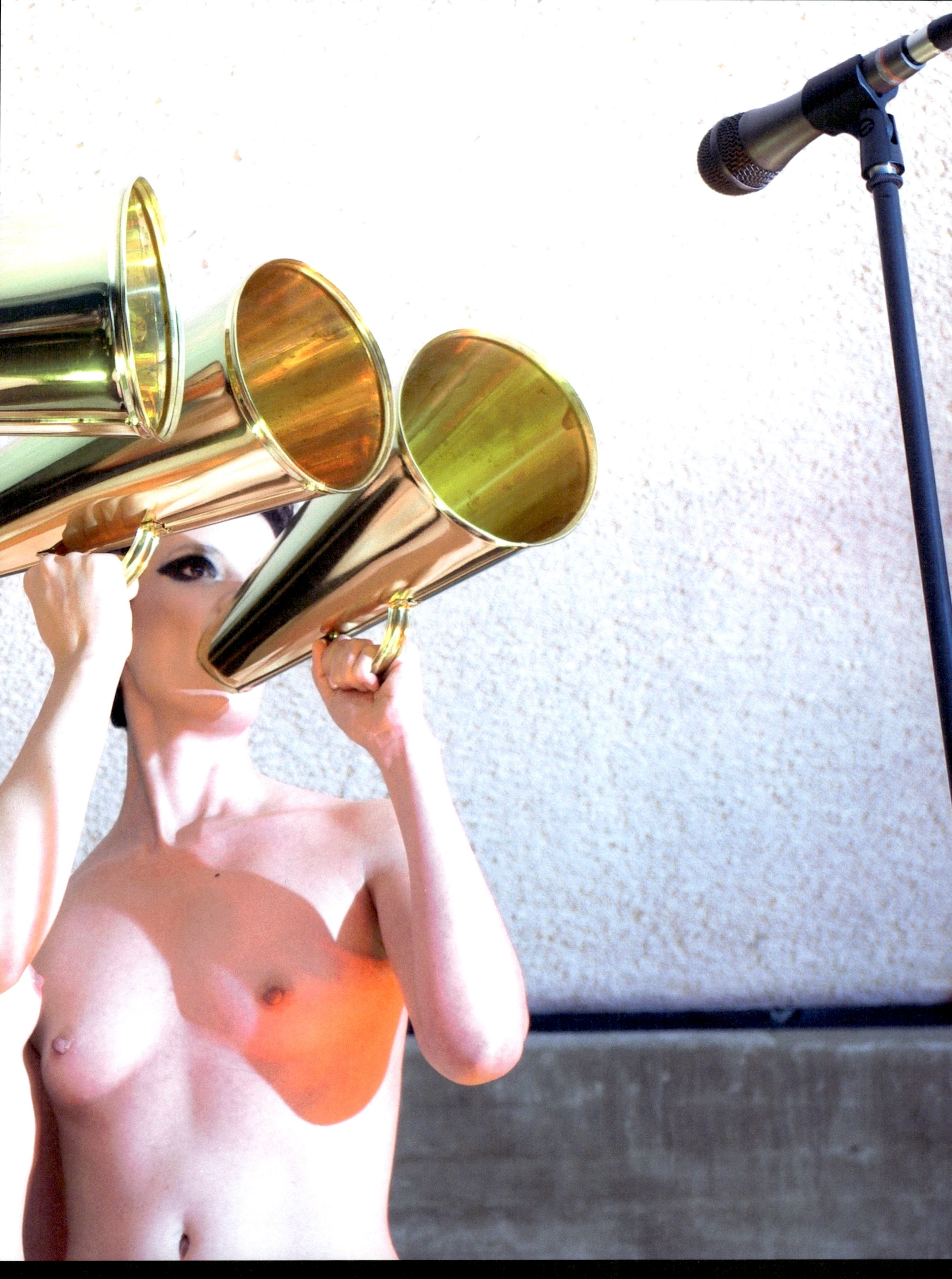

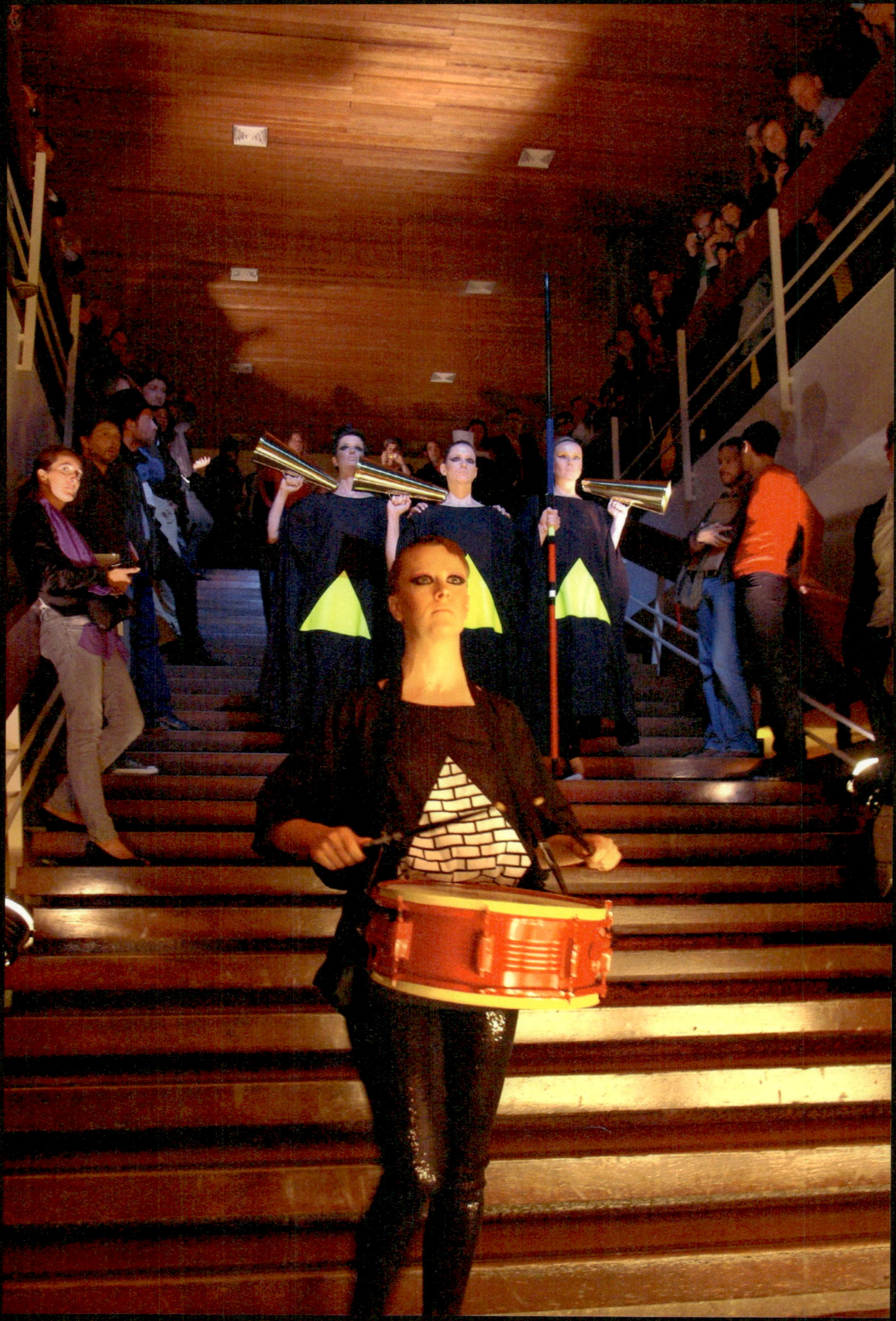

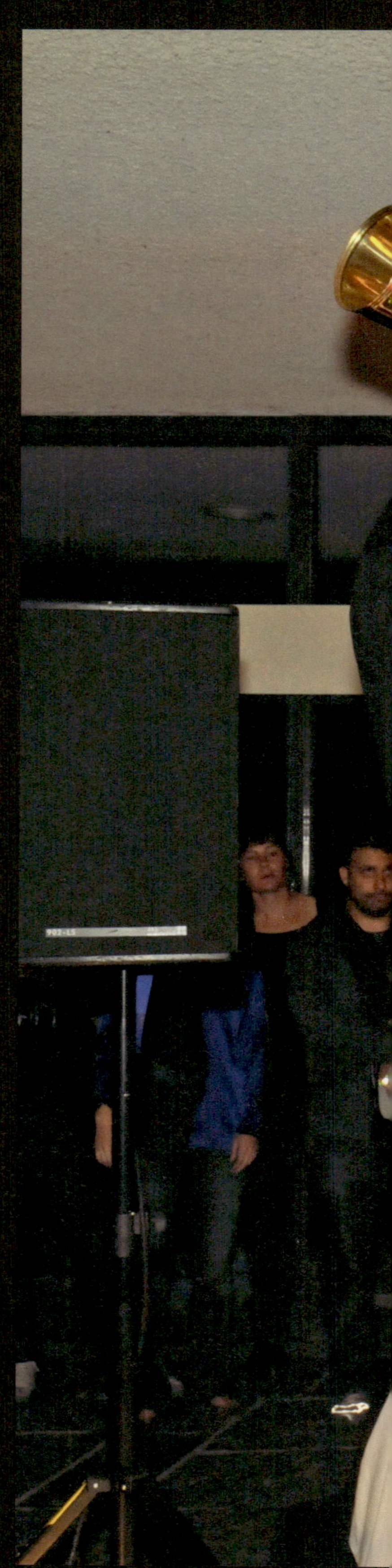

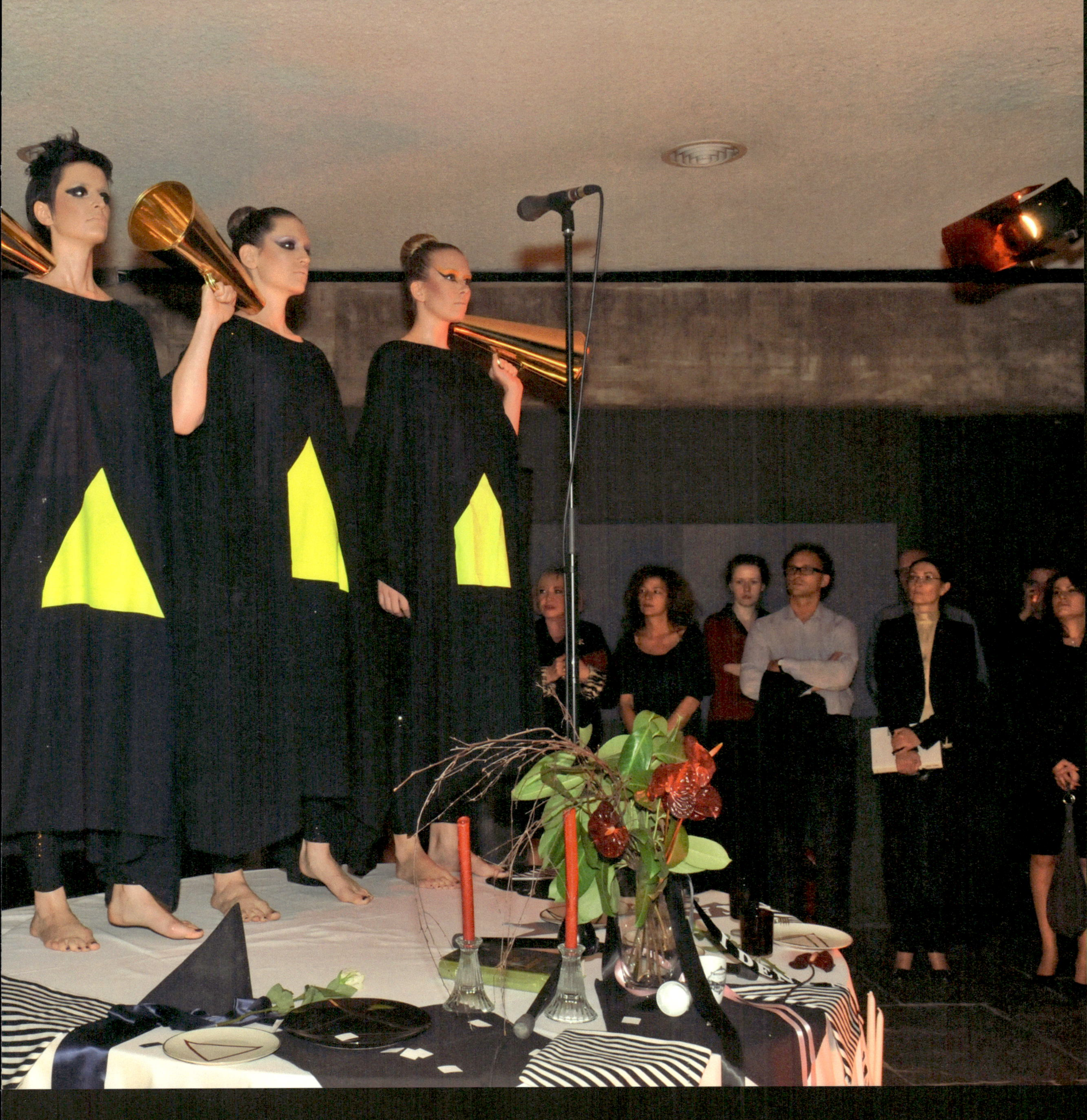

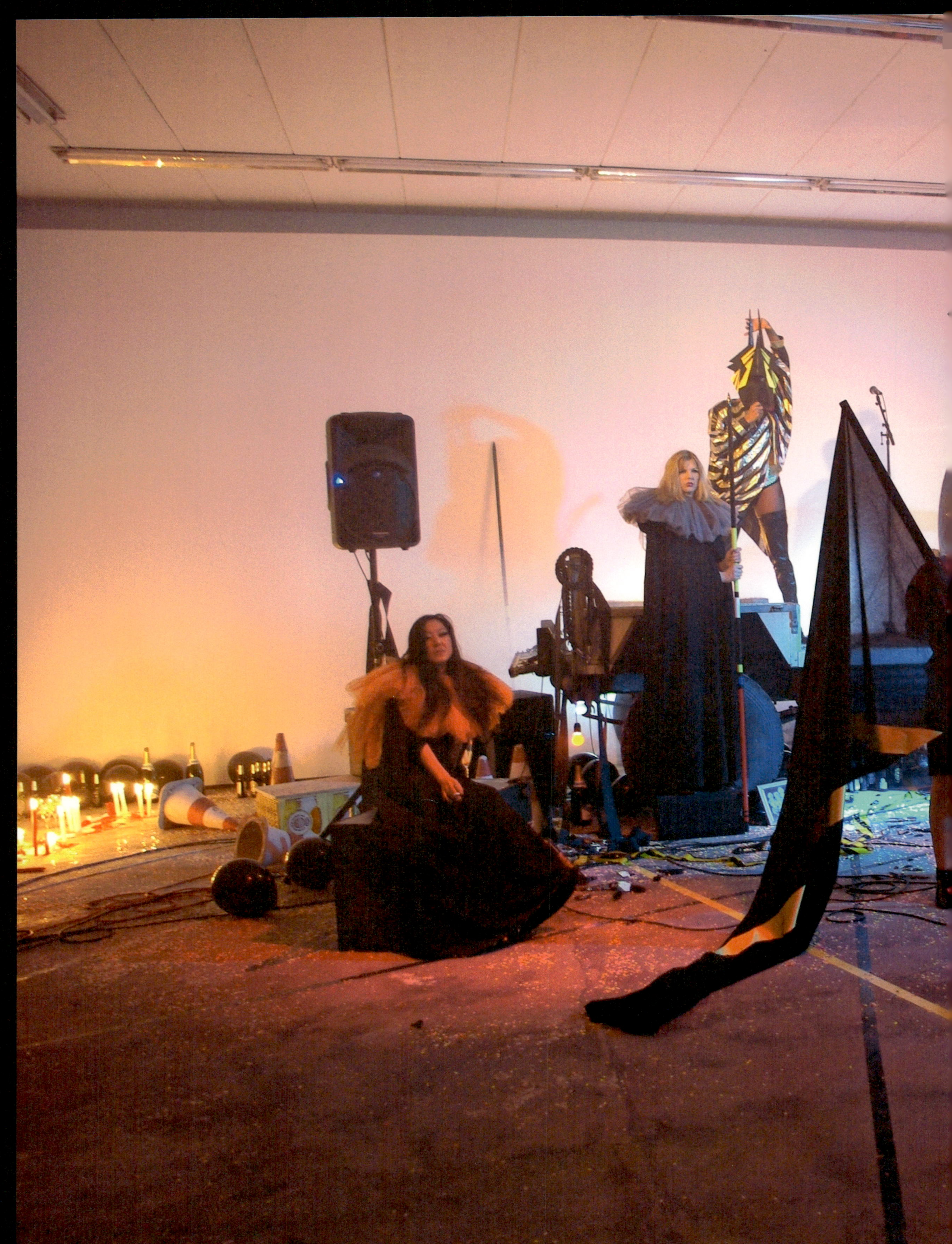

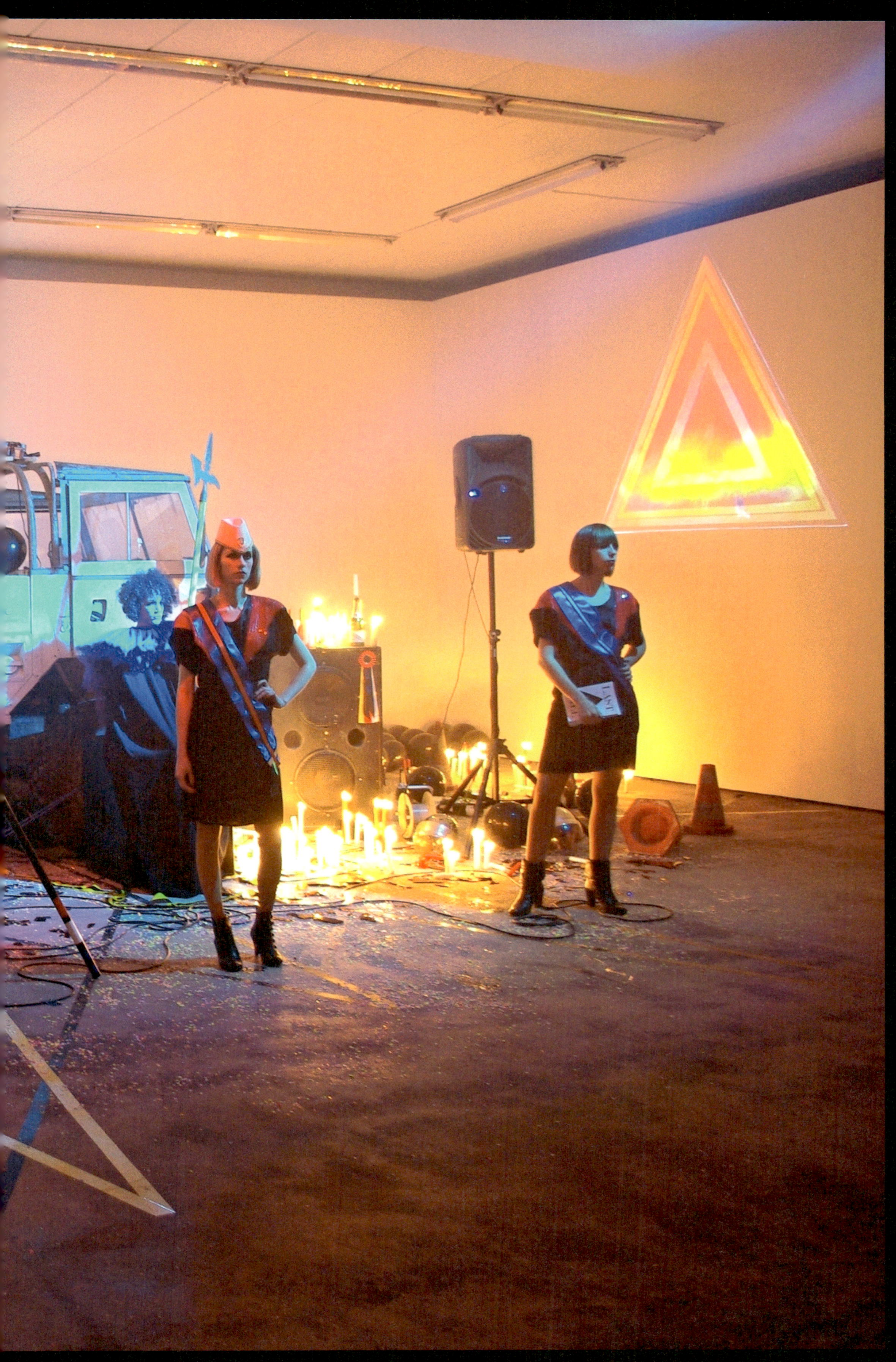

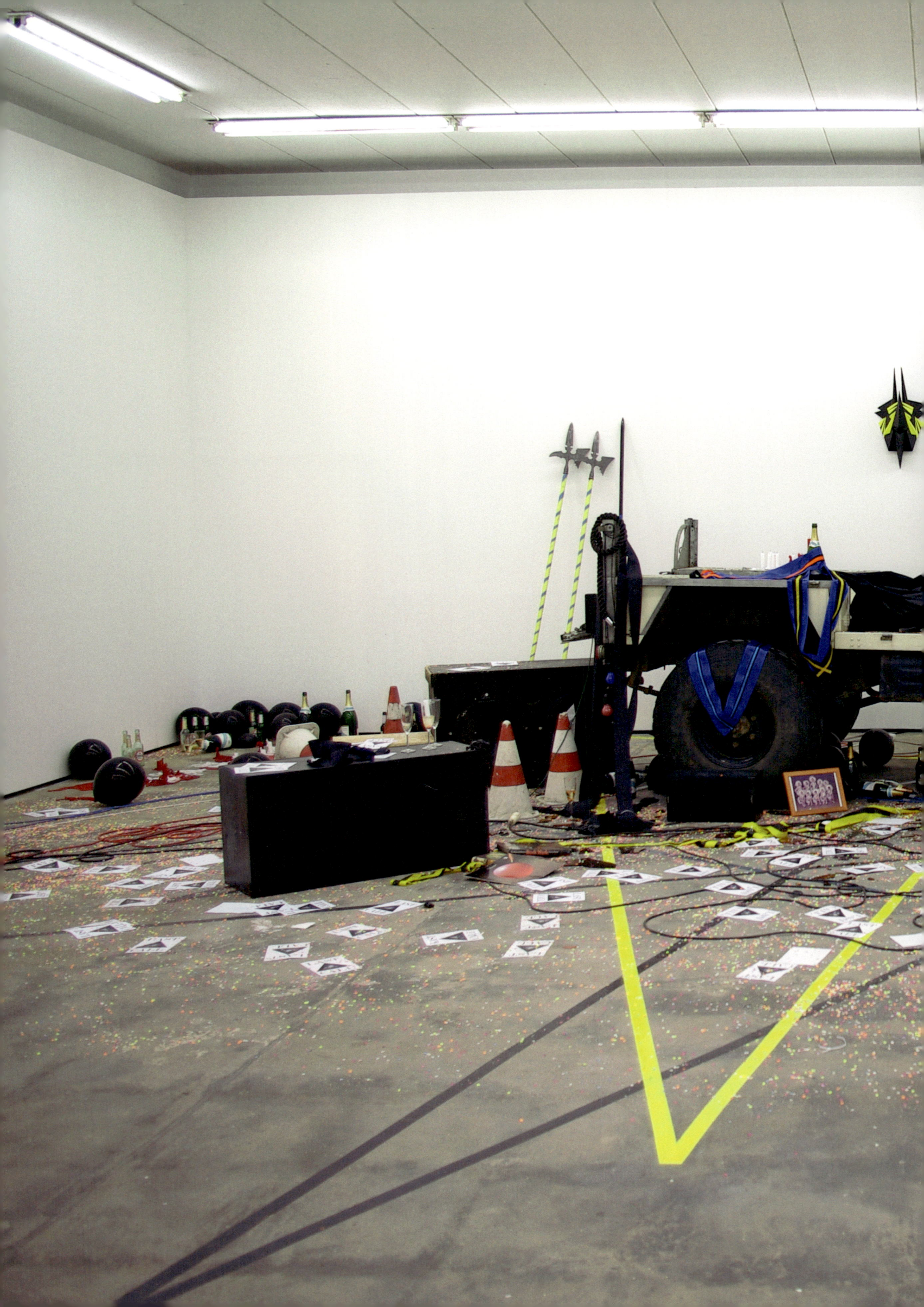

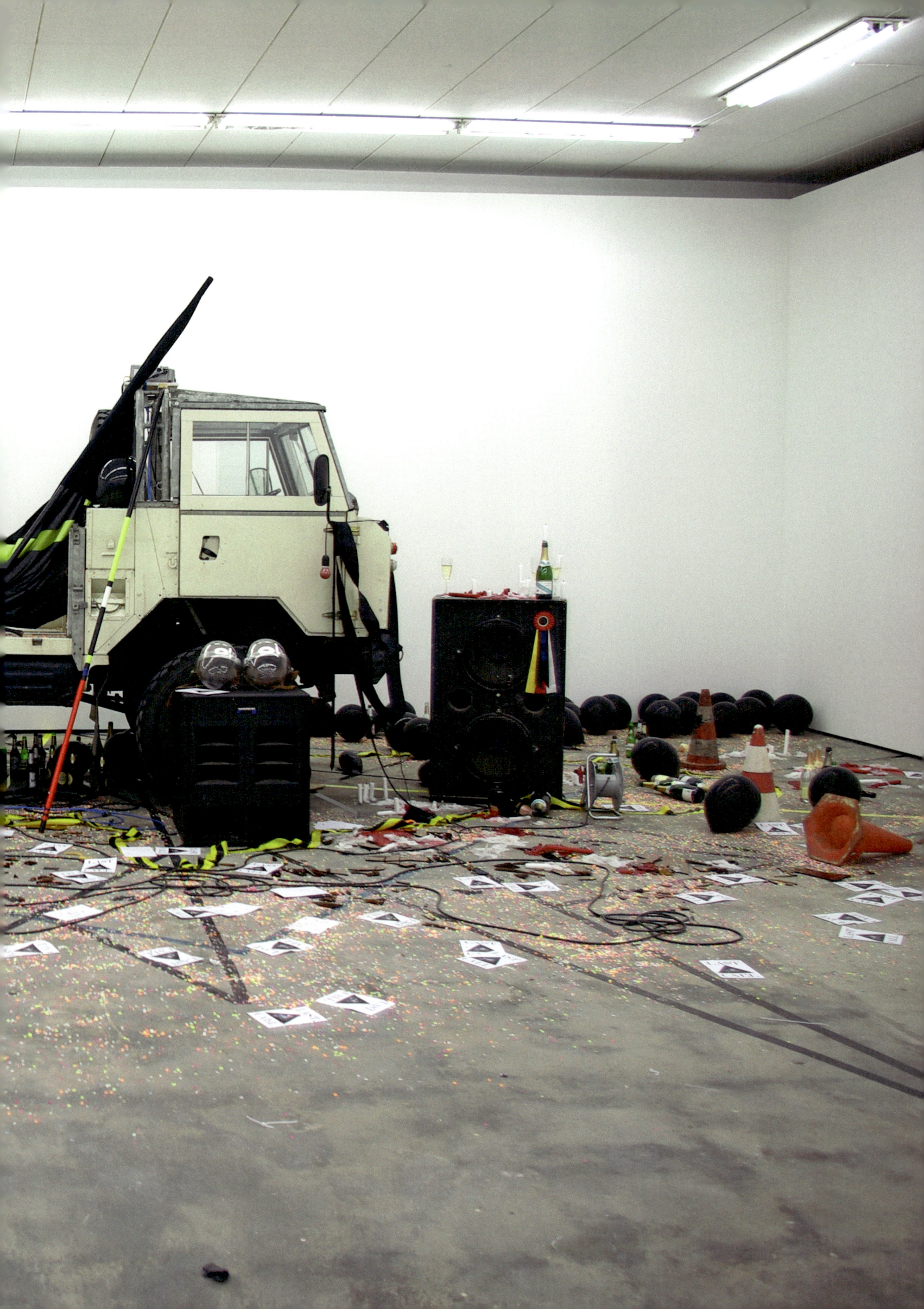

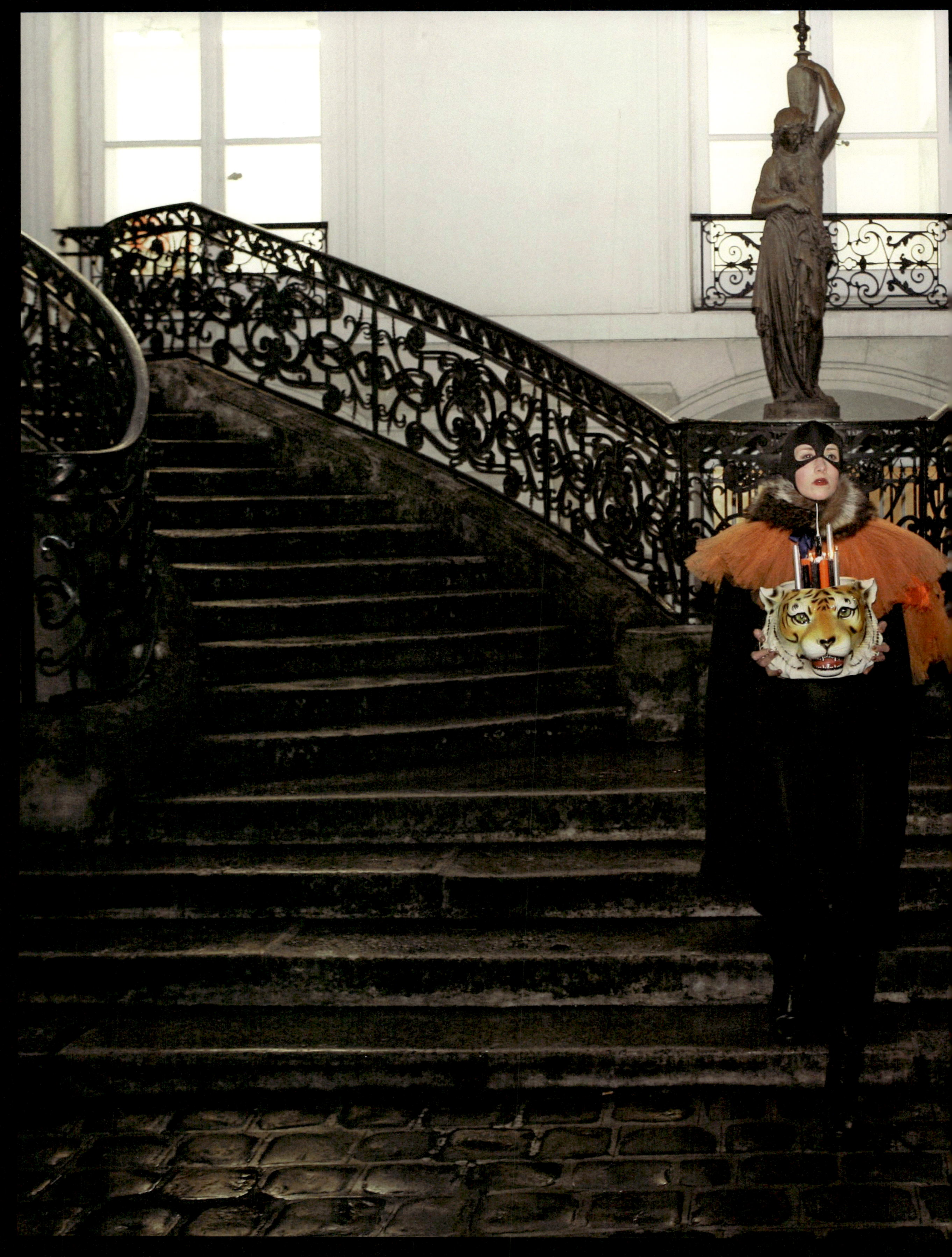

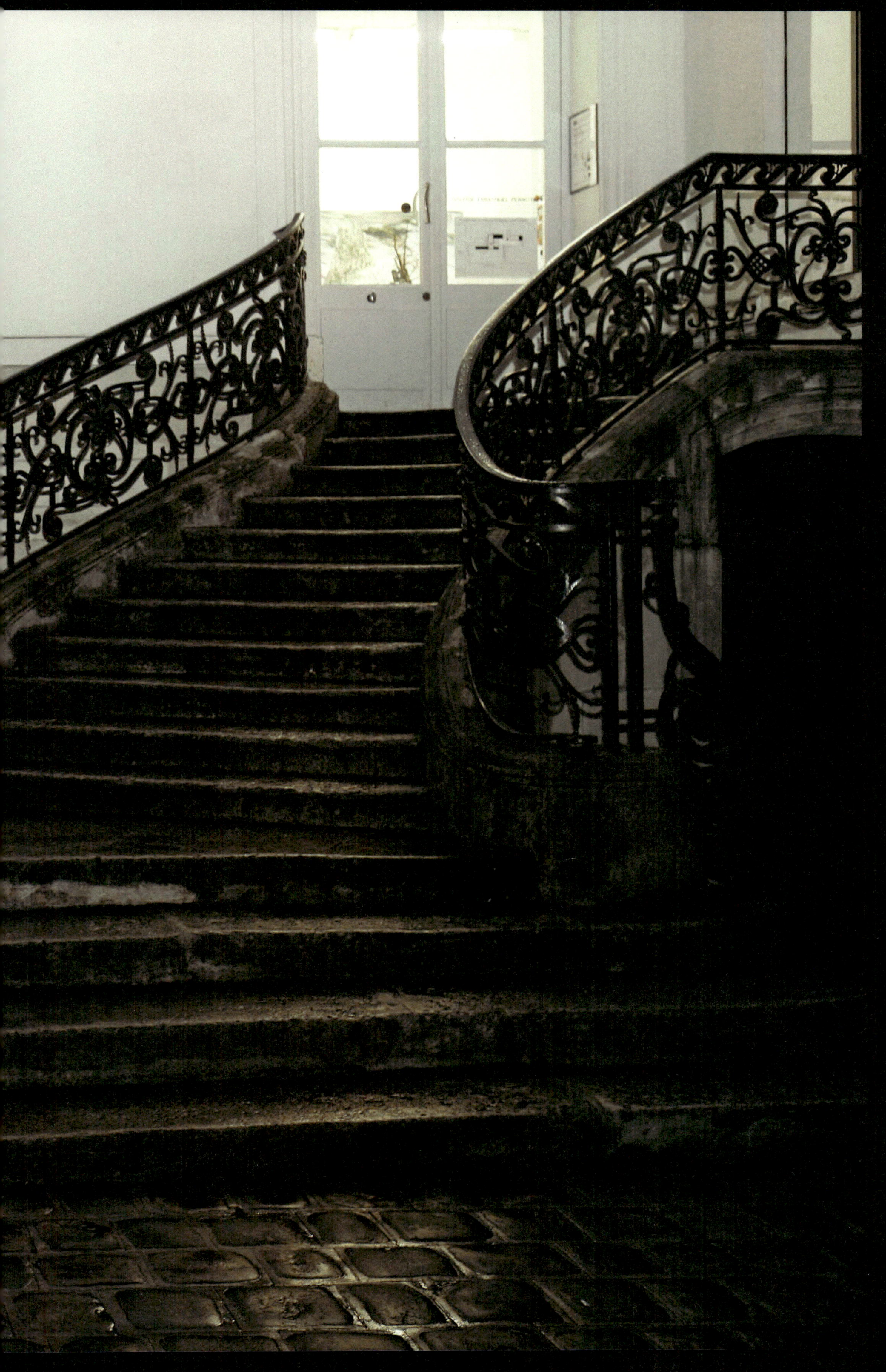

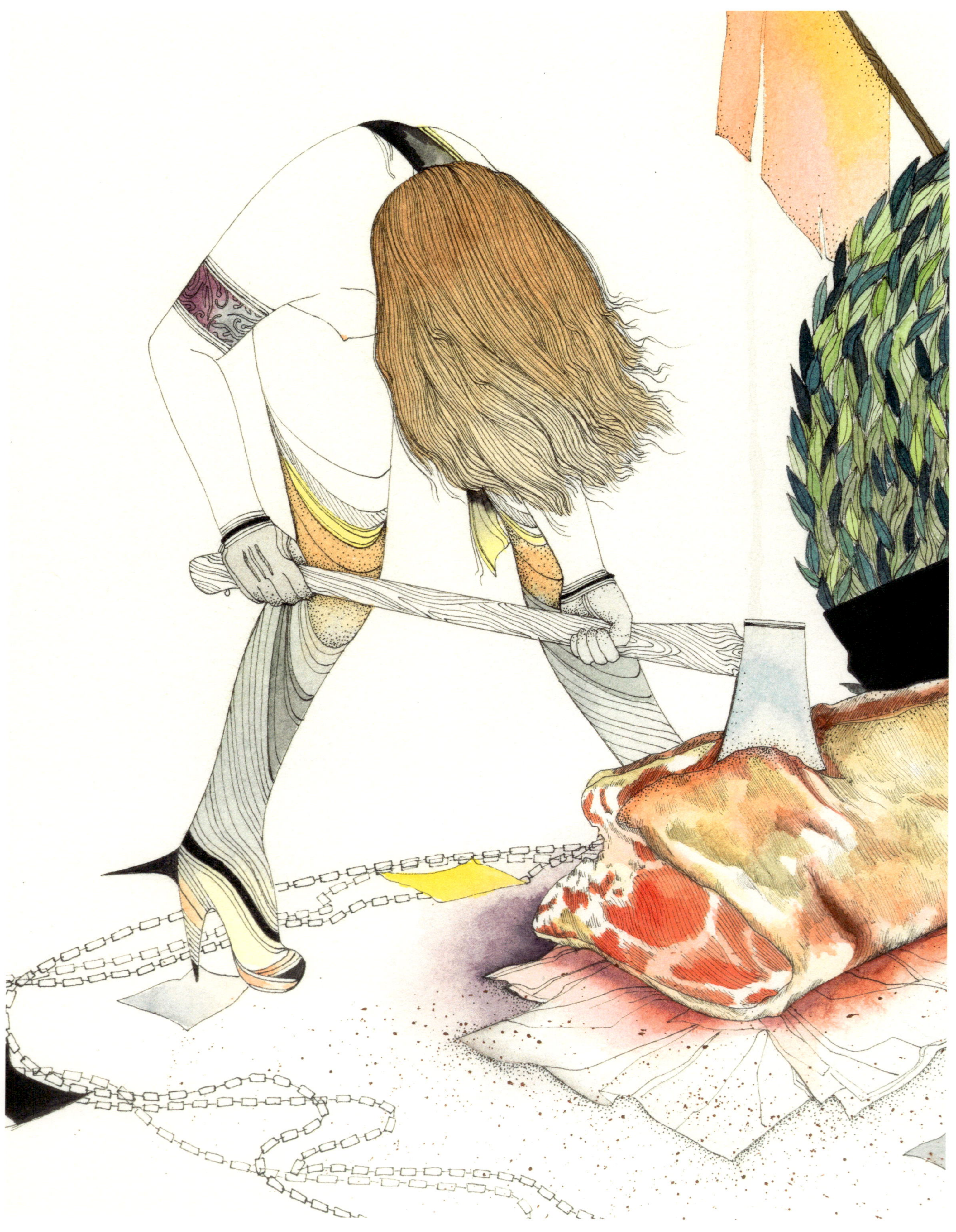

IMAGE INDEX

All images: Courtesy Wentrup, Berlin and the artist

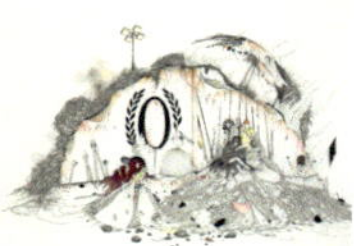

Untitled (The Year Zero), 2011
120 × 160 cm / 47 ¼ × 63 in.
Watercolor, ink on handmade paper
Private collection, Germany

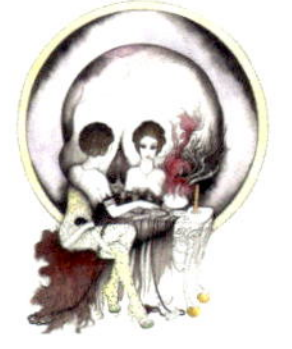

Untitled (Skull Woman), 2010
38 × 30 cm / 15 × 11 ¾ in.
Watercolor, ink on handmade paper
Pizzuti Collection, USA

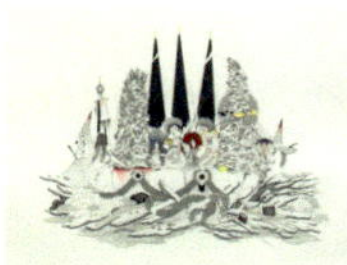

Untitled (The Last Supper), 2011
120 × 160 cm / 47 ¼ × 63 in.
Watercolor, ink on handmade paper

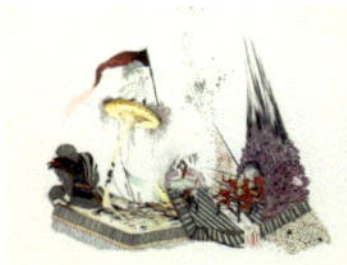

Untitled (Hairy Figure And Knights), 2007
120 × 160 cm / 47 ¼ × 63 in.
Watercolor, ink on handmade paper
Private collection, Germany

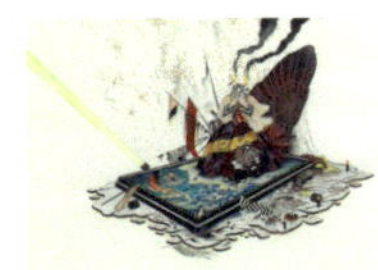

Untitled (Vampire Pool), 2008
120 × 160 cm / 47 ¼ × 63 in.
Watercolor, ink on handmade paper
Private Collection, Germany

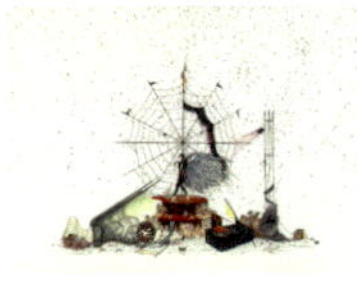

Untitled (Chain Stage), 2007
120 × 160 cm / 47 ¼ × 63 in.
Watercolor, ink on handmade paper
Private collection, Germany

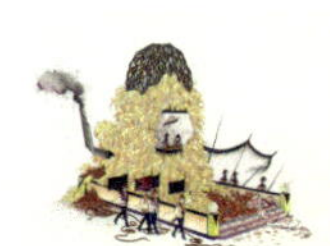

Untitled (Women With Flags), 2007
120 × 160 cm / 47 ¼ × 63 in.
Watercolor, ink on handmade paper
The Progressive Art Collection, USA

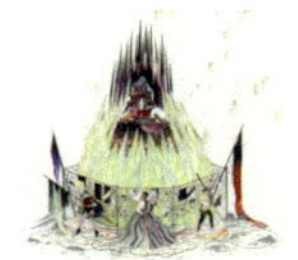

Untitled (Guarded Drums), 2007
120 × 160 cm / 47 ¼ × 63 in.
Watercolor, ink on handmade paper
Private Collection, France

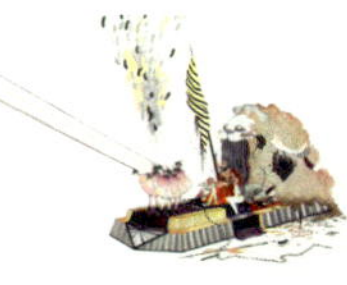

Untitled (Laser Float), 2007
120 × 160 cm / 47 ¼ × 63 in.
Watercolor, ink on handmade paper
Private collection, Switzerland

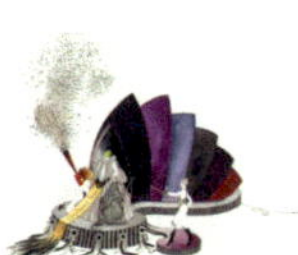

Untitled (Woman With Whip), 2007
78 × 105 cm / 30 ⅔ × 41 ⅓ in.
Watercolor, ink on handmade paper
Private collection, France

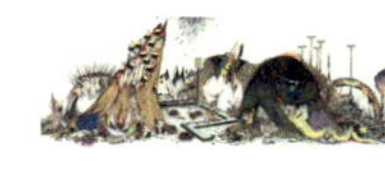

Untitled (Go Away), 2008
122 × 320 cm / 48 × 126 in.
Watercolor, ink on handmade paper
Gil Bronner Collection, Philara e.V., Germany

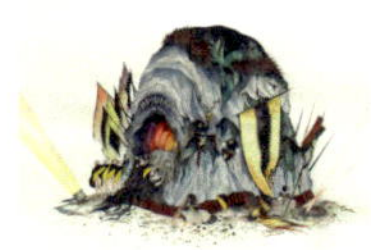

Untitled (Hi-Life), 2008
120 × 160 cm / 47 ¼ × 63 in.
Watercolor, ink on handmade paper
Private collection, Germany

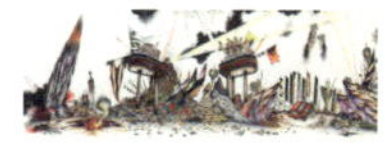

Untitled (Riot), 2009
122 × 320 cm / 48 × 126 in.
Watercolor, ink on handmade paper
Gil Bronner Collection, Philara e.V., Germany

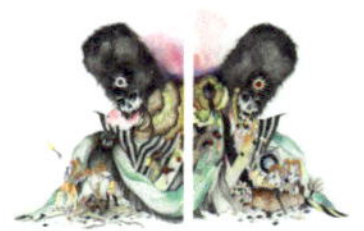

Untitled (Auto Da Fé), 2009
76 × 112 cm / 30 × 44 in.
Watercolor, ink on handmade paper
Gramann Collection, Germany

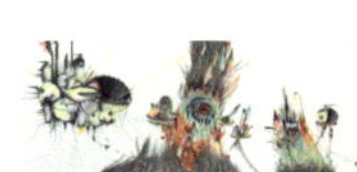

Untitled (Red Skull), 2010
122 × 320 cm / 48 × 126 in.
Watercolor, ink on handmade paper
Gil Bronner Collection, Philara e.V., Germany

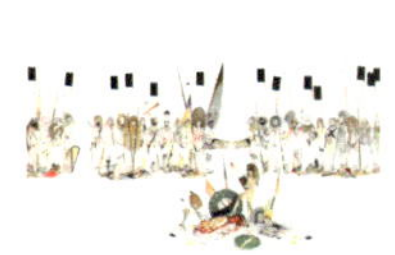

Untitled (Chorus Line), 2011
120 × 160 cm / 47 ¼ × 63 in.
Watercolor, ink on handmade paper

Untitled (No Surrender), 2007
76.3 × 57 cm / 30 × 22 ½ in.
Watercolor, ink on handmade paper
Angelika Taschen Collection, Germany

Untitled (Knight In Hole), 2007
76.3 × 57 cm / 30 × 22 ½ in.
Watercolor, ink on handmade paper
Private collection, Germany

JEN RAY

AIN'T WE GOT FUN

~

Edited by Jen Ray and Robert Klanten
Texts by Ana Finel Honigman and Robbert Roos

Cover by Jen Ray
Layout and design by Matthias Hübner for Gestalten
Typeface: Leitura by Dino dos Santos

Project management by Lucie Ulrich for Gestalten
Production management by Vinzenz Geppert for Gestalten
Proofreading by Bettina Klein
Printed by Livonia Print, Riga
Made in Europe

Photos courtesy of:
p. 63: Kai Dieterich; pp. 64-67: Melissa Hostetler; pp. 68-71: Franziska von Stenglin; pp. 72-75: Trevor Good; pp. 76-77: Guillaume Ziccarelli

Made possible by the support of Philara Sammlung Zeitgenössischer Kunst

Philara
SAMMLUNG ZEITGENÖSSISCHER KUNST

Published by Gestalten, Berlin 2012

ISBN 978-3-89955-437-3

For more information, please visit www.gestalten.com.

Bibliographic information published by the Deutsche Nationalbibliothek.
The Deutsche Nationalbibliothek lists this publication in the Deutsche Nationalbibliografie; detailed bibliographic data are available online at http://dnb.d-nb.de.

This book was printed on paper certified by the FSC®.

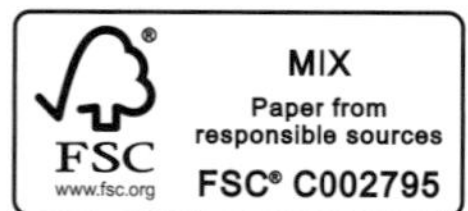

Gestalten is a climate-neutral company. We collaborate with the non-profit carbon offset provider myclimate (www.myclimate.org) to neutralize the company's carbon footprint produced through our worldwide business activities by investing in projects that reduce CO_2 emissions (www.gestalten.com/myclimate).

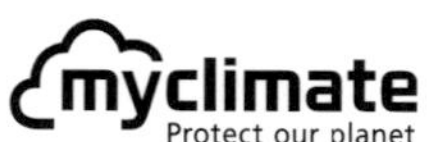